᠁ᵣ᠁ Reca᠁

CRIMINAL DANGEROUSNESS AND THE RISK OF VIOLENCE

Alfred B. Heilbrun, Jr.

University Press of America, Inc.
Lanham • New York • London

Copyright © 1996 by
University Press of America,® Inc.
4720 Boston Way
Lanham, Maryland 20706

3 Henrietta Street
London, WC2E 8LU England

Originally published 1989 by Westview Press

Library of Congress Cataloging-in-Publication Data

Heilbrun, Alfred B.
Criminal dangerousness and the risk of violence / Alfred B. Heilbrun,
Jr.
p.   cm.
Includes bibliographical references and indexes.
1. Violent crimes--Research--United States. 2. Danger perception--
Research--United States. 3. Criminal psychology--United States. 4.
Criminal behavior, Prediction of--United States. I. Title.
HV6789.H45   1996   364.3'0973 --dc20   96-19818   CIP

ISBN 0-7618-0408-0 (cloth: alk. ppr.)
ISBN 0-7618-0409-9 (pbk: alk. ppr.)

Contents

Preface

Crime, particularly violence, has increased to the point where it poses a serious threat to effective social order. It seems obvious that a clearer understanding of criminality in contemporary America would contribute to turning this unwelcome tide. Efforts to gain a better understanding may concentrate upon the broad issues of politics, class, and cultural values or the more focused concerns relating to the individual or predisposing situation.

My own interest has been directed to individual personality as it may influence the risk of crime and violence. The research has proven to be a valuable source of evidence that puts antisocial conduct into a different perspective. The theoretical model of criminal dangerousness that has evolved not only expands our understanding of criminal behavior but offers something of practical value. The evidence suggests that dangerousness can be measured, quantified, and then used to predict a number of undesirable outcomes that result in harm to victims or social systems.

The theory begins with the assumption that the predisposition to crime and violence is best considered in terms of multiple characteristics that may form a pattern. Two factors, antisociality and limitations in cognition, were studied to determine how well this combination could explain violent criminality. Evidence from studies described in this book suggests that dangerous criminality can be traced to generally flawed individuals who lack constructive social values but also are impaired in their cognitive functions.

Acknowledgement

To the Georgia Board of Pardons and Paroles whose continuing cooperation has made this body of research possible

Section I

Conceptual and Methodological Issues

CHAPTER 1

Conceptualizing Criminal Dangerousness and Criminal Violence

The problems of ever-increasing crime in the United States have been widely heralded by those who report the news or who otherwise offer social commentary regarding the corrosive effects of criminality. The suffering of the victims, the formidable job of apprehending criminals, the logistical difficulties of fair adjudication for those who are apprehended, the economics of incarceration for the guilty, and the conditions of prison release have all received considerable attention. Given a consensus that crime represents a formidable burden for our society, as well as most other societies, the appearance of a new theoretical model for criminal behavior based upon systematic research should be welcome. After all, from validated theory there could evolve important pragmatic gains, not the least of which might be an improved capability of anticipating who among us runs the greatest risk of future crime.

However, social science does not work that way. New theoretical proposals must contend with the skepticism of scientific colleagues who hold a different set of theoretical priorities that may not readily accommodate to the new proposal. At the same time, the vast army of professionals who must deal with crime at each stage--commission, adjudication, imprisonment, and parole--may lack enthusiasm for a theoretical proposal that has yet to be put to serious test in dealing with the day-to-day pragmatics of criminal justice. The reception given to any new conceptualization of criminal behavior depends to some extent on extraneous considerations as well. What is to be understood as criminal? Which crimes are to attract special concern at a given point in time? Is prison to be considered as a form of punishment, as a source of rehabilitation, or as a means of isolation? These issues are vulnerable to social and political winds that may shift without regard to scientific or professional input. What is considered dangerous criminality and how we should deal with it may shift as well.

The Case for a New Model of Criminal Violence

I shall try to anticipate any undue skepticism regarding the ideas and evidence to be put forward in this book by making it clear at the outset that the new theoretical model represents only a rudimentary explanation of crime and violence in personality terms. One way to gauge the immediate contribution of our theory and evidence is the extent to which they encourage the next, more formidable, stage of investigation. I shall lay out my view of what that research would involve before this book ends.

There are other factors worth considering when a new theory of criminality is introduced alongside existing explanations of crime in general and violence in particular. For one, the fact that the new entry seems only distantly related to extant theories should not in itself discourage careful consideration of the evidence and its potential heuristic value. I am convinced that the ultimate understanding of criminal behavior will require several theoretical models in order to accommodate the diversity of people who commit crimes and circumstances in which crime occurs. To some extent at least, we should encourage different theoretical assumptions about criminal behavior as long as we keep in mind that each theory must ultimately be empirically validated for the appropriate subset of criminals. This view that there is room for several criminal theories, then, requires that we entertain not only the question of whether a proposal fits the evidence but for whom?

The fact that the major emphasis in this book will be focused upon violent criminality leads me to suggest yet another reason why a new model that departs from existing proposals should be given careful attention. Any effort to fully comprehend violent behavior will likely require several levels of explanation. Seemingly different ways of conceptualizing why people display violence may result from whether understanding is approached in terms of biology, genetics, social-cultural influences, or personality. Rather than construing each approach as alternatives, they may represent different levels of explanation for the same phenomena. In the meantime, each theoretical camp should be open to the positions held by others.

As an example of explanatory levels rather than alternatives, dangerousness will be cast in personality terms in this book which would seem to set it apart from proposals that emphasize social class and culture as the backdrop for violence (e.g., Wolfgang & Ferracuti, 1970). However, there will be evidence presented that dangerousness in personality terms bears a relationship to lower-class membership in male criminals. It remains possible that the predominance of certain personality traits promoting dangerous behavior is a way of explaining why lower-class males contribute as much as they do to the statistics on violence. Personality and social class explanations are simply pitched at a different level of understanding.

A Meaning of Personality

I have remarked that the theory of dangerousness and violence that shall be presented in this book is a personality theory. This term has a number of surplus meanings and unfortunate implications that I shall try to avoid, but it does embrace the notion that an important origin of behavior is to be found in dispositional characteristics called traits. The supposition of personality traits bothers some social scholars and scientists, because they believe that the construct adds nothing to simply observing the behavior of the individual. They reason like this. You see a person behave in a particular way on a repeated basis. What does saying the person has a trait that disposes him to behave that way add to our knowledge or to our ability to predict? Just stick with the observed behavior.

I believe that a compelling case can be made for a personality-trait approach to understanding social behavior in general and criminal conduct in particular. Any trait theory serves to remind us that the primary origins of behavior are to be found in the behaving organism. While extrinsic environmental cues may occasionally be so compelling as to assume a dominating influence, for the most part the critical antecedents of a given act reside in the psychological processes of the individual. The only alternative to this view is a mechanistic assumption that we are controlled by our environment, a doctrine that has not received serious attention for many years. It is true that the means by which individuals instigate their own behavior are not well known, but the idea that the final functional responsibility for action resides with the person is beyond debate. If some type of action occurs with a degree of consistency, logic requires the source to be an enduring behavioral disposition--in other words, a trait.

The logic that compels a search for behavioral origins in the individual forms the backbone of any personality theory and that includes personality theories regarding criminal behavior. Yet what I propose as logical was not at all the prevailing view in forensic science during the 1970s and into the 1980s. For example, an antipersonality bias was evident in the warnings leveled by forensic scholars regarding the misuse of the term "dangerousness" as a descriptor of individual criminal risk. We are cautioned not to allow a risk-provoking characteristic of behavior to degenerate into a reified personality trait (Monahan, 1975); we are further warned to avoid a shortcut in definition from individual behavior as dangerous to the person as dangerous (Shah, 1978). Thus, the dangerousness of criminal behaviors was to be judged in terms of harm to the victim, but people who perpetrate these behaviors were not be considered dangerous in their own right. This was always a puzzling distinction to me, since it implies that someone is not dangerous in-between episodes of violent conduct. It makes more sense to assume that the person presents a risk of violence if he has engaged in aggressive behavior; risk pertains to the person and his behavioral dispositions.

It is hardly coincidental that many of the same scholars who considered dangerousness to be an unwelcome conceptual contrivance when proposed as a personality attribute also were strongly committed to an increased emphasis upon situational influences in predicting violent or otherwise dangerous acts. The assumption was that personality-based prediction had proven unsuccessful. The remedy was a return to a more balance consideration of the person-situation interaction both in terms of predicting violent action (Monahan, 1975; Shah, 1978) and other forms of social behavior (Mischel, 1973; Moos, 1973).

Since this book places heavy emphasis upon dangerousness as a personal characteristic that dictates individual potential for violence and lesser crimes, I think it important to offer a bridge between the skepticism of the 1970s and my own conviction that personality-based explanation for dangerous behavior holds real promise for understanding and prediction. It was certainly true enough that through the decade of the 1970s prediction of future violence received little assistance from measures of personality. This should have come as no surprise, since little else proved effective in anticipating future violence for specific individuals. I believe that the failure of personality data to make a more impressive showing in predicting crime and violence can be best understood in terms of an oversimplified technology of prediction and the low baserate nature of the events being predicted. As an example, the literature of that era reveals a number of studies of "psychopathic personality" as a unitary variable believed to be related to the proneness for violence. Some studies proved positive and promising (Davis & Sines, 1971; Hare, 1978; Persons & Marks, 1971), but the majority reported their own or earlier failures to establish a link between psychopathy and violence (Buck & Graham, 1978; Edinger, 1979; Gynther, Altman & Warbin, 1973; Kozel, Boucher & Garofalo, 1972; Levy, Southcombe, Cranor & Freeman, 1952; Panton, 1958; Wenk, Robinson & Smith, 1972). More laborious and complicated efforts to establish complex personality patterns that might stand a better chance of successfully predicting violence were the exception. In short, the serious limitations of a personality approach in predicting or postdicting violence seem just as readily explained by oversimplified procedures than by the limitations of a personality strategy.

Besides being committed to a personality approach to understanding and predicting crime and violence for logical reasons, I am equally impressed by the heuristic value of a personality emphasis. Because of the multidisciplinary character of forensic science in which psychology, psychiatry, sociology, criminology, biology, law and other disciplines play contributing roles, a variety of research approaches have been brought to bear on the issues of criminality. Which of these varied disciplines maintains the most profitable strategy of research remains unsettled. It does seem fair to observe, however, that systematic research within any discipline is conducive to progress whatever the preferred strategy might be. Systematic here refers to programs of research in which one study evolves from another in order to implement a coordinated strategy of investigation, to address questions that have been raised by previous investigation, and to replicate earlier results. Systematic study implemented by a program of research stands a better chance of gathering the kind of evidence necessary to develop and validate a theoretical model of criminal behavior. The variety of personality variables that are accessible to measurement and the option of studying them in combination provide a vast resource ideally suited for systematic investigation.

A Definition of Terms

The importance of defining terms is especially vital when understanding criminal violence is at issue. Violence is one of a family of terms (violence, dangerousness, aggression, force, crime) that have been assigned varied meanings, so that it becomes difficult at times to align the findings of one researcher with those of another. This book will not improve the general state of the literature, since I intend to introduce my own set of meanings for these terms that may depart in some respects from other efforts. However, by being explicit in meaning and consistent in usage, I hope to avoid confusion within my own writing. First I will touch upon the state of the literature as far as the meaning of important terms is concerned and then provide a working vocabulary for this book.

Examination of the meanings assigned to the term violence by forensic scientists reveals a core of agreement that this type of behavior results in physical injury to another person or, at least, intends or threatens such injury (Megargee, 1976; Pasternak, 1975; Rubin, 1972; Sampselle, 1992). The use of force to accomplish injurious ends has been emphasized by some in defining violence (Brizer & Crowner, 1989; Monahan, 1981; Stuart, 1981), but the term, taken to mean exerting power against another person's will, introduces its own brand of imprecision. If a man physically overwhelms a woman and rapes her, it is readily understood as the use of force to achieve a violent end. What if the woman readily submitted to being raped for fear of suffering more serious injury. Does the force of intimidation differ from physical force, and in what way is the violence of the act altered? Others have extended the meaning of violence beyond actual or intended injury to another by force to include damage to property or personal reputation or even illegal appropriation of property. Casting the conceptual net this broadly makes the meaning of violence essentially synonymous with criminality and makes one term or the other redundant (Ervin & Lion, 1969).

Dangerous behavior is commonly used to refer to violent action (Brizer & Crowner, 1989; Megargee, 1976; Pasternak, 1975; Shah, 1977). This usage flirts with the assumption that the only crime conveying real harm to a victim is one that involves or threatens physical injury. When used as synonymous with violence, the dangerous quality of crimes also becomes redundant and dispensable in its usage. I discussed earlier in this chapter that both Monahan (1981) and Shah (1977) objected to the vagaries of the term "dangerousness" as it shifts the emphasis from criminal behavior to a hypothetical attribute of the criminal. To this point, then, we have encountered little value for the term "dangerousness" within the forensic literature.

Aggression has been the concept of choice in other attempts to understand crimes of violence. Goldstein (1975) defines aggression in much the same way as others--behavior intended to physically injure another person--but he includes psychological injury as a goal of aggression as well. Once you include both physical and psychological injury to a person in the definition of aggression, the equation of violent crime to aggressive crime is thrown out of balance. Crimes that include the psychologically injurious threat of physical harm, such as robbery, are violent; crimes that involve other psychologically injurious behaviors, such as burglary that deprives people of their personal possessions, are aggressive but not violent. Others have avoided the pitfalls of trying to equate criminal aggression and violence by considering one as an extreme form of the other. Valzelli and Morgese (1981) considered violence to be a pathological extreme of aggression resulting from heightened arousal of brain mechanisms. In a similar vein, Gunn (1973) maintained that aggression was the more general attacking process and took violence to mean severe aggression.

The manner in which the various terms will be employed in this book will share as much common meaning as possible with the community of definitions that have been discussed to this point but will include some clear-cut points of departure. Let me begin with the term dangerousness that I intend to use as a characteristic that is represented to a variable extent across all criminals. This will be recognized as the traditional approach to understanding personality constructs. My usage never departs from essential dictionary meanings; danger is an exposure to harm, and harm refers to hurt, injury, or damage. To be in danger, then, is to be at risk or in peril. Dangerous describes the source of risk and its capability of doing harm. Dangerousness, in turn, would allude to the intrinsic properties of a person, object, or situation that would threaten someone or something with harm.

As used in the theoretical context of the multifactorial model that will be presented, dangerousness refers to characteristics of the individual that place others at-risk for harm through criminal behavior. The term criminal dangerousness is as broad as the term criminality, but the two are not synonymous by any means. The former is a psychological term based in personality designating the degree of harm that the person might potentially inflict upon a victim through criminal action. The latter is a quasi-legal term often used to describe the person's commitment to crime. Crimes will differ categorically with regard to implied dangerousness of the criminal; as an example, rapists are more dangerous than child molesters, because they tend to inflict more serious physical and psychological harm upon the victim. However, a given category of criminals, when examined closely, will show a range of dangerousness judging by their offenses. Some rapists (and child molesters) are more brutal in their sexual aggression than others committing the same criminal offense.

The dimension of criminal dangerousness is construed as extending from the circumscribed harm to victims (other than the criminal) that results from "victimless" crimes and from most forms of property crime to the serious harm of psychological trauma and physical injury that follows from the more severe violent crimes. Conceptualizing dangerousness as a dimension may not represent an altogether novel approach to understanding the risk of harming others that distinguishes one criminal from another. However, the introduction of criminal dangerousness as a personality dimension within the theoretical model of crime and violence to be proposed is somewhat more unique.

Conceiving dangerousness as a continuous individual-difference variable serves as a valuable research tool in that it encourages the researcher to go beyond the limitations of categorical distinctions. Rather than settling for either-or typologies like violent/nonviolent criminality to establish gross distinctions in dangerousness, investigation is more likely to go into specific nuances of crime and seek a more precise calibration of the risk variable. In order to achieve these research advantages, two methodological requirements must be satisfied. One of these involves the identification of individual-difference variables that would allow the researcher to represent dangerousness as a personality characteristic. It was necessary for me to break away from using past crimes as the metric of dangerousness, although they continued to serve a valuable function as one of the major criteria by which theoretical validity of the model was to be judged. The way that the criminal dealt with the victims of his past crimes should show some correspondence to assessed dangerousness.

Once the personality variables constituting dangerousness are identified, the second requirement involves their translation into some form of measurement and quantification. As discomforting as it may be to render something as complicated as the potential for criminal harm to a single quantitative score, this was the only way I knew to introduce any real precision to the statistical analysis of research data that was to be collected. I knew I could not depend upon the ponderous numbers of single-study demographic research to establish reliability of my findings, nor was I tempted to use case-study inquiry that eschews statistics for more complete revelation in a few selected cases.

The scientific value to be realized by bringing criminal dangerousness out from under the operational shadow of past crime did not become fully apparent until the program of research had been underway for many years. I already have mentioned the advantage of being able to use past criminal conduct as a validating criterion of dangerousness rather than as its operational definition. It also was apparent at the outset of research that establishing the dangerousness of a given criminal as near to the time of his inclusion in a study would provide a more relevant metric. Without exception, the index of criminal dangerousness that was adopted for our research was a more proximal measure than the crime that led to incarceration and availability as a subject. The crowning realization came, however, after we had enough research behind us to understand that dangerousness shows up in different behavioral guises. That is, highly dangerous criminals would have the more violent criminal history as expected, but they also displayed greater criminal risk in terms of recidivism, maladjustment on parole, and prison misconduct. However, dangerous criminals tended to demonstrate one but not another of these criteria of dangerousness. If criminal history had been the choice for defining dangerousness, it is unlikely that we would have gained broad insight into the dangerous criminal.

The use of the term <u>violence</u> in this book will remain close to the meaning employed by earlier writers. Violent crimes will include those that involve actual physical injury and attendant psychological distress or the risk of physical harm. I do not include the use of force as a requisite for violent action, although physical force or verbal intimidation is commonly found. One reason that I do not require force as a prelude to violent crime is that I choose to include all sexual crimes involving physical contact as violent. There are cases in which sexual acts involving physical contact are not forced upon the victim. Child molestation and incest may occur by seduction, gentle persuasion, or even degrees of cooperation on the part of the child. Effects on the young victim may be devastating even though physical force was not involved.

Violent behavior and dangerous behavior are treated as related but not synonymous terms. The greater harm to victims resulting from violent behaviors leads me to expect that violent criminals will fall toward the higher end of the dangerousness dimension and that property offenders will assume a lower position. The assumption of dimensionality presumes that all violent criminals would not be expected to show equal dangerousness and that nonviolent criminals would also be spread over a range of values. More harmful violence (e.g., murder) should be displayed by more dangerous criminals and less harmful violence, as far as physical harm is concerned at least (e.g., child molestation), should be associated with less dangerous criminals. Intentionality also would be expected to play a role in determining dangerous outcomes as an act causing maximum harm (death) could be completed without intent. Unintentional homicide (e.g., involuntary manslaughter) would be treated as evidence of a less dangerous predisposition than willful killing.

Nonviolent crimes should be perpetrated by less dangerous criminals, since they generally result in limited harm to the victims. The inclusion of all criminals on the dimension of dangerousness, however, acknowledges that nonviolent criminals also harm their victims and are dangerous because of that. The expectation that criminals who engage in violence will be found in the upper reaches of a dangerousness dimension does involve the assumption that physical well-being is more important than property and possessions. Said another way, I assume that the suffering and anguish resulting from physical injury is more harmful to the victim than repercussions of nonviolent crimes.

The Working Model for Criminal Dangerousness

The original two-factor hypothesis of dangerousness (Heilbrun, 1979) was proposed as an approach to predicting criminal violence from a personality perspective that might improve upon previous efforts that had attracted such criticism during the 1970s. I reasoned that too much had been expected of personality predictions in the attempt to anticipate a low base-rate event like violence. It was noted, for example, that personality formulations tended to be either too simple, as in single-variable predictions, or the variables in more complex predictions were not sufficiently relevant to violent outcomes. Before relinquishing a commitment to personality prediction of violence, I recommended that this procedure be given a better chance to succeed by selecting relevant variables and using them in combination. The study reported in this 1979 paper represented a demonstration that violence became more predictable when two personality factors, relevant when considered together, were employed.

The first factor that was chosen for investigation in the 1979 study was antisociality, the tendency to violate the mainstream society's values regarding human conduct. Antisociality may take the form of criminal acts that breach the formal laws of society, although it is hardly restricted to illegal behavior. Other expressions of antisociality are to be found in the lifestyle choices and social misconduct that flaunt the value systems that are popularly held by the broader society. These more popular values define what represents mutually-satisfying and reciprocally-fair social interaction, constructive goals, and the social institutions that form the fabric of society. I recognize that the issues of adherence to law and value in diverse 1995 America are more complicated than this treatment of antisociality suggests. Departure from mainstream values may involve the adoption of constructive alternatives. It is when behavior is contingent upon defiant rejection, simple ignorance, or destructive alternatives that antisociality as a construct is merited. Both the law and value systems are broadly recognized (if not followed) in American society, and the extent to which they are respected or ignored represents a legitimate, though complex, personality dimension. Antisociality, then, is treated as an individual characteristic that helps determine the likelihood that legal and moral restraints of the mainstream society will be breached.

The second personality factor that I considered in the effort to relate personality to violence was a coalition of cognitive deficits that would be conducive to ineffective transaction with one's social and physical environment. Although the critical cognitive functions remained a matter for speculation in 1979, impairment in reasoning, judgment, planning, social insight, and the cognitive underpinnings of self-control were considered to be of likely importance.

My rationale for the combined importance of antisociality and flawed cognition in explaining dangerousness and in the prediction of criminal violence followed along these lines in the two-factor proposal. Antisociality confers a risk for committing a criminal act, since the moral restraints that deter such conduct in most people are not effective and self-control is generally lacking. Although these criminal acts may involve the intent to commit or at least threaten physical violence, for the most part the intended illegal act will not. However, the risk of violence increases when the antisocial person lacks the ability to plan, reason, or judge beforehand how such an act might be consummated without placing a victim at-risk for physical injury. In addition, the criminal may not be able to deal effectively with those who are present at the crime scene, because he lacks the experience or other cognitive skills to do so. The risk of physical violence escalates, because the interaction between the criminal in control and the victim is more likely to deteriorate in socially-unskilled hands.

Accordingly, my reasoning presumed that bungled planning of criminal acts and ineffective transaction with the victims of crime may turn nonviolent intent into a violent reality. Even if the intended crime requires contact with a victim and is violent on the face of it, as is true for rape or robbery, deficits in socially-relevant cognition introduce a likelihood of escalation to an even more serious level of violence in which the victim is brutalized or killed. The combined relevance of the two personality constructs was simply this. Antisociality made it more likely that the individual participated in a criminal act, and cognitive limitations increased the likelihood of bungled planning and deteriorating social transaction.

The two factors, antisociality and cognitive deficit, were proposed as independent but as having an interactive relationship to criminal dangerousness and violence. When antisociality and cognitive deficit co-exist, the person falls high on the dimension of dangerousness and is at greater risk for violence. Level of dangerousness and the risk of violent crime are expected to drop given any other combination of antisociality level and cognitive competence. If antisociality serves to determine the probability that a criminal act will occur and cognitive deficit contributes to the risk of violence toward a victim of that act, high antisociality combined with better cognitive skills or low antisociality coupled with impaired cognition would not be associated with the same level of risk for the victim. Low antisociality and better cognition completed the possible psychological pairings and were assumed to represent the lowest risk for serious harm to the victims of crime.

This dangerousness proposal was never intended to explain all types of crime and every show of violence toward a victim. Although I initiated research on the two-factor model of criminal dangerousness by lamenting the simplification of personality approaches to prediction, I recognize that the shift from univariate efforts to a two-variable interactional strategy is not a profound one. By considering only antisociality and cognitive competence, I was far away from exhausting the individual psychological characteristics that might impact upon the harmfulness of human conduct. Situational context, biological factors, and genetic influence were also to be ignored as the research progressed. Acknowledging the obvious, everything cannot be studied at the same time. Nevertheless, I have found myself continuously surprised that so much supportive evidence, collected from so many perspectives related to crime, has been generated by what became the two-factor model of dangerousness. Readers, of course, will have to judge for themselves how broadly applicable and how convincing this psychological explanation of dangerousness appears to be.

Another caveat must be issued, and then we can move on to the research on dangerousness and the evidence it has produced. I have presented an argument for the combined importance of antisociality and cognitive impairment in explaining criminal behavior in general and violence in particular. To do this, antisociality has been assigned a major role in determining whether criminal acts will occur, and cognitive impairment has been proposed as responsible for bungled planning or incompetent criminal transaction with the victim that introduce increased risk for more serious harm to those who are the targets of crime. I have no doubt that these two factors can contribute to dangerousness in just the opposite way. A person may be more likely to commit a crime if he suffers from cognitive limitations, and the same person may escalate harm to the victim as the crime progresses because of his poorly developed value system. Even so, the combined presence of antisociality and cognitive flaw would represent the greatest danger to other people. I will adhere to the original rationale for dangerous criminal conduct, because it would be too laborious to continue equivocating on the functional roles played by antisociality and impaired cognition every time the subject of how dangerousness translates into victim harm arises.

CHAPTER 2

The Methodology of Research

Sixteen years have elapsed since publishing my first investigation of a two-factor model that seeks to explain criminal dangerousness and, at its extreme, the risk of violence. Data continues to be collected as this book is being written in an effort to test as many nuances of the model and to provide as much validation as possible before presenting it to a wider audience. The program of research responsible for extending and validating the model has brought with it a number of methodology considerations that require examination. This chapter will provide that opportunity.

Quantification of the Antisociality/Cognitive Impairment Pattern

The two-factor hypothesis regarding criminal dangerousness required that a psychological pattern be introduced into the search for validating or elaborating relationships. There were two ways in which this requirement was satisfied within our research designs, and each served its purpose in the program at different stages.

Early in the program (Heilbrun, 1979; Heilbrun, 1982; Heilbrun & Heilbrun, 1985) the scores of the antisociality and cognitive effectiveness measures were distributed independently and a median (middle score) split on each variable was used to designate high and low levels. This approach compelled our use of the dangerousness pattern as the independent variable for purposes of analysis. More specifically, it involved the comparison on some behavior of interest between four gross categories of criminals who fell theoretically at three levels of dangerousness. These levels ranged from high dangerousness (high antisocial-low cognitive effectiveness) through intermediate dangerousness (high antisocial-high cognitive effectiveness, low antisocial-low cognitive effectiveness), to low dangerousness (low antisocial-high cognitive effectiveness). Criteria or correlates of dangerousness were allowed to vary freely as dependent variables.

The employment of antisociality-cognition patterns as independent categorical variables had its limitations. Even though it proved valuable in encouraging continued research when validating relationships were uncovered early in the program, two shortcomings were clearly in evidence. The first of these is inherent in any effort to represent continuous dimensions as categories. There is a loss of discriminative power around the cutting-points that define the categories. For example, if antisociality were measured as a continuous variable on a scale from 0-100 and the middle score of the sample of subjects were 55, a two-category split might define a subject scoring 56 as "high" on the variable and another scoring 55 as "low." There are ways of getting around this problem of unreliable assignment to groups by eliminating subjects around the mid-point from the analysis. The more you eliminate, however, the less the research sample is representative of a meaningful population to which one can generalize results. Eliminating subjects also reduces sample size and lessens the confidence you can have in your findings.

The second limitation of the categorical-pattern approach followed in the initial studies was the inflexibility of requiring that the dangerousness dimension be employed as the independent variable. There would be greater leeway in research design if dangerousness could be introduced either as an independent or a dependent variable. Allow me to illustrate the difference. If, as in the second study of the program (Heilbrun, 1982), there is an interest in whether dangerousness relates to self-control, the use of a categorical-pattern approach made sense. Criminals, split into the three levels of dangerousness offered by dichotomous categories, were compared in terms of several continuous self-control scores. However, it would have made just as much sense in this study if self-control had been categorized into levels, such as better and poorer, and dangerousness had been introduced as the dependent variable. If there were a continuous score representing dangerousness rather than categories, this choice would have been available as would data analysis procedures in which both variables under scrutiny would best be continuous (e.g., product-moment correlation).

The value of greater flexibility in how we were to deploy

dangerousness within our analyses is especially obvious if the variable being related to dangerousness were inalterably categorical and would be most profitably employed as the independent variable. Several studies that shall be reported in the next section of this book considered the severity of certain crimes and the relative dangerousness of the men who commit those crimes. Whether men are burglars, rapists, robbers, or murderers does not translate into a meaningful continuous score that might serve as a contingent dependent variable. Given a continuous score representing degree of dangerousness, these criminals could be subjected to a more sensible analysis in which criminal types are compared on their relative potential for harm to their victims. The availability of a continuous score given this approach to validation of the dangerousness model allowed for more powerful parametric statistical analysis of the data. Otherwise, less precise nonparametric statistics involving two categorical variables and frequency counts would have been required. Sometimes the availability of a more powerful statistic can make a difference in the process of discovery, especially if subject numbers do not reach very high figures.

A quantitative index representing degree of dangerousness within the two-factor model was introduced as a solution to the limitations of categorical assignment. I chose an unweighted multiplicative function in which the dangerousness score was the product of two more specific scores designating degree of antisociality and degree of cognitive impairment. The two components of the index were assigned equal weight, because I had no theoretical basis for assuming one to have greater priority than the other in promoting dangerousness. The choice of a multiplicative function for combining the two scores was appropriate but arbitrary; a voice from my graduate student days and exposure to Hull-Spence learning theory prompted me to multiply the terms. I could have added the scores and achieved the same end.

The mechanics of producing the dangerousness score based upon antisociality and cognitive components went like this. The distributions of raw scores for both components were transposed in each study to standard-score distributions with a mean of 50 and a standard deviation of 10. This allowed each criminal in a particular sample to be assigned a dangerousness score by multiplying his antisociality standard score by his cognitive-impairment standard score. The fact that each component score is derived from the same type of standard-score distribution assures equal weighting for the two variables. The hypothetical average dangerousness score following such a procedure is 2500, the score generated by a subject who falls at the sample mean of 50 on each of the standard-size distributions. Actual sample dangerousness means might vary from this number depending upon how skewed the raw score distributions might have been or other idiosyncracies of the data.

The interpretive implications of this quantification procedure are straightforward as long as you recall that antisociality and cognitive deficit are represented by higher scores on their respective component distributions. Subjects who would have fallen into the "high dangerousness" category using the original system of categorizing subjects (above the median on both scores) automatically have high scores on the continuous quantitative index. For example, scores of 60 on antisociality and 60 on cognitive deficit would provide a very high index score of 3600. By the same token, those who would have had lower, below-median scores for categorical assignment would necessarily have lower index scores. A subject with factor scores of 40 and 40 would be represented by a very low index score of 1600. The intermediate-dangerousness categories (high antisociality-low cognitive deficit, low antisociality-high cognitive deficit) would feature a wide range of index scores depending upon the extent that the two factor scores departed from the sample medians in different directions for a given subject. To illustrate, if subject A provides an antisocial score of 51 (high) and a cognitive-impairment score of 35 (low), overall dangerousness would be quantified at 1785. Subject B, who might have been identically classified by the original category procedure, offers a tandem of scores comprised of 70 and 49 and an overall dangerousness score of 3430. This hypothetical comparison of two subjects, identically classified by one scheme but with scores varying from 1785 to 3430 provided by the other, portrays vividly why the multiplicative index score offers a more precise specification of dangerousness than categorical assignment.

Measurement of Antisociality and Cognitive Impairment

Antisociality. My original conceptual focus in addressing the issue of complex personality predictions of violence was upon psychopathy (psychopathic personality). This construct had, to that point, a rather bleak predictive record when considered alone; I questioned whether psychopathy might fare better as a predictor if considered in combination with a second type of personality variable. My nomination, of course, was impaired cognition (Heilbrun, 1979).

I relinquished the construct of psychopathy as suitable to my theoretical interests in the 1980s and chose instead to adopt the term "antisocial" to describe the value factor in my model of dangerousness. The reason was simple enough. There were too many characteristics thought to define the psychopath that were extraneous to the theoretical notion of dangerousness that was under consideration. Clinical consensus at that time described psychopathy as a personality disorder based upon failed socialization in which the individual shows deficiencies in loyalty, guilt, and frustration tolerance along with a selfish, callous, impulsive, and irresponsible life-style (American Psychiatric Association, 1968). In addition, egocentricity (Arieti, 1967; Foulds, 1965; Hare, 1970; Karpman, 1961) along with absence of interpersonal emotion (Cleckly, 1964; Craft, 1965; McCord & McCord, 1964) had received considerable emphasis in describing the psychopath. Antisociality, as the preferred construct, placed singular emphasis on one aspect of this complex personality pattern -- "a repeated and flagrant disregard for social customs and mores " (Dahlstrom & Welsh, 1960). Such disregard obviously would carry over into violations of legal constraints. Antisociality, then, provided a suitable and sufficient conceptual basis for predicting the occurrence of criminal conduct within the dangerousness model.

The psychometric measure of antisociality that was used in many of the dangerousness studies included two scales; one was selected from the Minnesota Multiphasic Personality Inventory (MMPI; Hathaway & McKinley, 1951) and the other from the California Psychological Inventory (CPI; Gough, 1957). The MMPI Psychopathic Deviate (Pd) scale was developed by selecting those items within a larger item pool that discriminated between a largely-delinquent criterion group and normals. The delinquents had shown a lengthy history of "stealing, lying, truancy, sexual promiscuity, alcoholic overindulgence, forgery; but no capital offenses..." (Dahlstrom & Welsh, 1960, p.61). The nature of this criterion group and fact that my own experience in prison assessment confirmed some degree of elevation on this scale for all types of criminals convinced me that the Pd scale was suitable as a measure of antisociality.

Concern about the limited power of any one self-report personality scale led to the addition of a second scale that was to be used in combination with Pd for measuring antisociality. The CPI includes a Socialization (So) scale that considers the extent to which the individual has adopted the values of the greater society. The So scale was originally devised to cast additional light upon psychopathy (Gough, 1957), so it shares that much in common with the Pd scale. However, the rationale for derivation of the So scale differed in that the emphasis was upon the role-taking deficiency associated with this personality disorder. The behaviors correlated with high So scores as reported by the manual (e.g., honest, conscientious, responsible, conforming) and with low scores (e.g., resentful, headstrong, rebellious, undependable, and guileful and deceitful with others) testify to the appropriateness of using the So scale as an added measure of prosocial and antisocial tendencies. A recent review of the research evidence concerning this scale corroborates the merit of low scores as an indicator of the "flawed internalization of social norms" (Gough, 1994, p.692).

There is an overlap of items between the Pd and So scales, but since this figure was less than 20%, I anticipated that each scale could add something to the measurement of antisociality independently of the other. The procedure for using these self-report personality scales in unison was guided by the mechanics of scoring on their respective questionnaires. Antisociality is reflected by higher scores on the Pd scale and by lower scores on the So. Accordingly, the subtractive index of Pd-So provides an indication of antisociality with each scale contributing appropriately. Either an increase in Pd or a decrease in So adds to the algebraic value of the final antisociality score. The fact that both questionnaire scale scores are distributed with a mean of 50 and standard deviation of 10 allows equal weight to be given to each scale in the raw antisociality scores. As I have already discussed, these raw difference scores are then transformed to a standard-score distribution before being entered into the dangerousness index.

While this psychometric approach to measuring antisociality seemed to work well, as gauged by theoretically consistent results across studies, it did introduce some procedural requirements that eventually led me to employ an alternative method in order to expand our sources of data. When the data required for a particular study had been generated as part of parole assessment procedures in which consultants were assisted by staff of a prison diagnostic center, the time-consuming individual administration of both the MMPI and CPI was possible. Accordingly, whenever Pd-So antisociality scores were used, they had their origin in parole assessment proceedings. Many studies, however, depended upon prisoner files for research information, and files never included questionnaire results that we could use. This made it necessary to devise an alternate measurement procedure for antisociality that could be scored from standard file information abstracted and rated by research technicians.

Before providing greater detail regarding the second antisociality measure, I would like to point out that the alternate did help resolve one of the limitations of the questionnaire approach. Both the MMPI and CPI are standardly administered as self-report measures with the subject responsible for reading each item and selecting the "true" or "false" response. Administration of these tests to a prisoner was subject to a 6th grade reading level on the Wide Range Achievement Test (Jastak & Jastak, 1965) as a way of precluding nonreaders from taking these inventories and providing random responses. Since lack of reading skills is going to be heavily represented among the least intelligence prisoners, the use of self-administered tests that require reading will tend to bias the sample selection toward more intelligent prisoners. For example, the average IQ of prisoner samples has reached as high as 107 when the 6th grade reading requirement was maintained. Other studies, using filed information that did not impose this requirement because a different antisociality scoring procedure was used, saw the IQ mean drop almost 10 points.

The bias toward higher intelligence found in studies that incorporate the MMPI and the CPI and require some reading skills actually worked against finding validity evidence in support of the dangerousness model. The IQ is taken to be an important marker of higher mental processes such as planning, reasoning, judgment, social insight, and empathic understanding, and these cognitive functions contribute theoretically to criminal dangerousness by their absence. By precluding nonreaders and mostly low-IQ criminals, it is likely that the more clear-cut cases of cognitive impairment were ignored in some of our research. Nevertheless, theoretical support for the dangerousness model was consistently apparent in the questionnaire studies despite having to truncate the range of cognitive impairment. This suggests the power of the theory may be underestimated by those studies.

The alternative method for measuring antisociality was reported first by Heilbrun & Gottfried in 1988. When criminal case histories served as the basis for establishing antisociality rather than individual assessment by questionnaire, the diagnostic criteria for antisocial personality disorder recommended by Feighner, Robins, Guze, Woodruff, Winokur, and Munoz (1972) were adapted for this purpose. The nine criteria of antisocial personality proposed by Feighner and his group included: (1) school problems (e.g., truancy, fighting), (2) running away from home, (3) police problems (e.g., multiple arrests), (4) poor work history, (5) marriage problems, (6) repeated outbursts of rage or fighting (not in school), (7) sex problems (e.g., serving as a prostitute or pimp), (8) vagrancy, and (9) repeated lying or use of an alias. Evidence for any of these behaviors in the criminal's social history or police record would point toward antisociality as a personality disorder.

It was considered preferable to use probability rating scales for each criterion rather than categorical present/absent ratings in light of the uneven amount of relevant information found in case files for prisoners. There were times when nuances of information would allow conditional judgment but not categorical certainty. Accordingly, a 4-point probability scale was completed by a judge for each criterion of antisociality gauging the likelihood that the problem behavior was represented in the criminal's past. The evidence was rated from 0 ("definitely not"), through 1 ("possibly") and 2 ("probably"), up to 3 ("definitely"). In line with the probabilistic character of the ratings, the highest score of 27 would mean that the evidence definitely portrayed the criminal as antisocial. The lowest score of 0 just as definitely dismissed antisociality as a characteristic.

Looked at in another way, the high score represents the judgment of a rater that the given criminal has definitely displayed each of the nine types of antisociality in his history. The low score follows from an equal certainty that none of the specific antisocial behaviors was in evidence within the history of the criminal in question. Extreme scores are more than probability statements then; they tell us in a more absolute way that the criminal has been pervasively antisocial or has been fully cognizant of social values. Intermediate scores by this line of reasoning depict the criminal as antisocial in some ways but not in others. A check on the reliability of the ratings, in terms of interjudge agreement, revealed a high correlation of r=.87 between independent raters in the 1988 study. Despite the sometimes obscure character of prisoner files, the information on the backgrounds of criminals allows for excellent agreement between judges.

Cognitive impairment. The necessity to generate thousands of prisoners as subjects for the program of studies that will be considered in this book, along with the limited availability of research personnel, placed serious restrictions upon individualized measurement of subject behavior. Staff members at the Georgia Diagnostic and Classification Center, Jackson, Georgia, assumed the responsibility for individual administration of the psychometrics that were required for my research program. However, as I have explained, they did this as part of a program of parole assessment in which I participated and not for assistance in my research. In short, there was no way in which I could have arranged for the extensive time, space, and personnel required for individualized measurement of cognitive functions. Accordingly, I had to adopt a marker of impaired cognition from what would be routinely available for prisoners in the state of Georgia.

The IQ score from a standard intelligence test was adopted for this purpose based upon the assumption that lower intelligence would be associated with curtailed cognitive skills and higher intelligence would signal an improved quality of cognition. This assumption seems clearly warranted. If you examine the concept of general intelligence and the manner in which this construct is popularly measured, the higher mental processes that are represented include cognitive functions such as planning, reasoning, and judgment. These also are cognitive functions I have identified as critical in their absence within the dangerousness model.

I would not suggest that a unitary IQ score offers an ideal way of depicting an array of cognitive functions; a more demanding assessment of individual cognitive skills that would establish a cognitive profile for each criminal would have been preferable. That certainly will be one of the recommendations that I shall make as the evidence from the research program is discussed in the final chapter. However, since the logistics of research dictated that only the IQ would be available as a rough estimate of cognitive skill, it seemed preferable to proceed on that basis in testing my ideas than to remain on the sidelines for lack of perfection. If the theoretical model of dangerousness can accrue convincing evidence of validity using IQ as a rough marker of cognitive effectiveness, then more demanding (and expensive) research would be called for.

The IPAT Culture Free Intelligence test (Scale 2; Cattell & Cattell, 1958), a nonverbal measure of Thurstone's general intelligence factor, has been employed as the source of IQ scores throughout the program of research. This instrument is used as part of a standard assessment battery administered to criminals entering the prison system in the state of Georgia. The IPAT test is considered especially valuable as a means of bridging the diverse cultural and educational backgrounds of the prisoners. Early research demonstrated the reliability and validity of this intelligence test, especially Scale 2 (Cattell, 1940; Cattell, Feingold,

& Sarason, 1941), and subsequent review substantiated its superiority among culture-free measures (Jensen, 1972).

Subjects Under Investigation

Subjects who were studied as part of the dangerousness research program were convicted felons in the state of Georgia and had been incarcerated within the prison system of that state. The one exception was an investigation of patients found not guilty of their crimes due to insanity in which scarcity of subjects made it necessary to obtain additional data from the state of Florida. A high majority of the subjects in the program of research were males, and for that reason the dangerousness model is considered to have its more immediate applicability to men. However, some efforts were made to test the model across gender lines, so the female criminal was not ignored in our investigation of dangerousness.

The criminals under investigation were adults almost without exception, only occasionally including late teenagers. Prisoners over 60 years were also rare. Samples varied in mean age from a low of 26.27 years to a high of 32.96 years. Average educational attainment over these samples fell between 9.32 years and 10.44 years with individual schooling ranging from no formal classroom work to a graduate-level education. Racial proportions of white to black prisoners within the research samples varied from a roughly 2:1 ratio to about equal representation. The few hispanic prisoners collected in our samples were included in the white grouping when race was considered. No criminals of an oriental racial origin were represented within our subject pool as far as I know. Socio-economic backgrounds were predominately lower-class; one probe found 58% of the male prisoners to be from a lower-class background and 42% were considered middle-class.

Procedures of Investigation

Studies within the dangerousness research program employed one of two methodologies that already have received some comment. Some studies focused upon men who had been selected for psychological assessment to assist the Parole Board in making a decision regarding prison release. This often resulted because the Parole Board had some serious questions relating to risk of endangering new victims when paroled. At other times, psychological assessment as a prelude to release was imposed as a requirement by the court at the time of sentencing. When prisoners were to be assessed they were transported to the diagnostic center for Georgia's Department of Corrections where they remained for a week. During this time they were given a battery of psychological tests including the Culture Free Intelligence Test, the Wide Range Achievement Test, and (if they obtained a 6th grade reading level) the tandem of personality tests--the MMPI and CPI. Tests were administered by the staff of the diagnostic center's testing section over a 1-2 day period. Review of social and prison history, along with an interview by a psychologist, completed the assessment.

There are both scientific pros and cons associated with this method of data collection. On the plus side, all subjects being assessed received the psychological instruments under remarkably similar circumstances of physical setting, testing personnel, and subject motivation. Standardized testing conditions, then, were to a large extent realized. It was also fortunate and not surprising that Parole Board and court concerns about parole risk were often leveled at men with a history of violent crime. This proved providential, since it allowed access to more substantial samples of violent criminals, especially dangerous ones at that. Violent criminality was a primary research interest.

The major drawback to the evidence collected as part of a parole assessment is the prevailing motivation of the criminals to look good for the Parole Board. This is, of course, what you would want for estimating intelligence and cognitive effectiveness; impaired cognition should be apparent despite the prisoner's best efforts on the test. Personality testing could be more cause for concern as far as dissembling is concerned. My clear-cut impression though is that dissimulation had little systematic effect upon the MMPI and CPI and the Pd-So antisociality score except to add slightly to the difficulty of discrimination between prisoners. This would only work against finding positive results in those studies involving questionnaire data and make validation of the dangerousness model that much more difficult.

Perhaps the greatest reassurance regarding the possible effects of response sets upon the Pd-So antisociality index is that results based upon this score and those based on the multi-criterion ratings of antisociality taken from social and criminal histories fed into the same theoretical model without a hint of discord. The former could have been influenced by response set of the prisoner but the latter could not, yet they both served (in liaison with IQ) to validate the proposed understanding of criminal dangerousness.

The second method of data collection that was utilized in some of the studies involved random selection of cases from the files of the Georgia Board of Pardons and Paroles rather than using prisoners referred for assessment. Usable files always contained the Culture Fair IQ score and the personal history data necessary to complete the antisociality ratings. This approach promised a sample of cases more representative of the general prison population with regard to intelligence, since it was not necessary to exclude nonreaders. The rates of nonviolent and violent criminals available for study also were in line with prison population proportions. File search was the research methodology of choice when the issues under investigation had to be scrutinized by detailed data embedded within the criminal files. This information would not have been available from individual criminals, at least in reliable form. Judgmental ratings were often required, such as degree of brutality involved in a crime, so that the evidence could only be collected with the assistance of raters within a setting in which their research participation was permissible. The Georgia Board of Pardons and Paroles was unstinting in their cooperation throughout the research program.

The limitation of the file research method for us is the same as that inherent in all file-based methodologies. It is a static procedure so that investigation is restricted to whatever happens to be standardly included in the folders of prisoners. Although some cases are inevitably found to be unusable for research purposes, this did not present much of a problem. For one thing, when file research was undertaken, we only went after information in the records that stood a good chance of being included. Simple demographics, criminal history, circumstances of the most recent crime of record, and parole performance (if relevant) are standard features of the criminal's record. The sheer number of available criminal records is another reason why eliminating a case from investigation presents no problem. Criminals are not scarce in Georgia or anywhere else for that matter.

Section II

The Validity of the Dangerousness Model as a Predictor of Criminal
Violence and Recidivism

CHAPTER 3

Validation of the Dangerousness Model Based Upon Between-Crime Comparisons

Criminal dangerousness, as I have defined the term, represents the risk of committing a criminal act that results in harm to one or more victims. Perhaps one of the reasons why the use of dangerousness as a risk factor may prove to be so vexing is that the probabilistic connotations of the definition can make reference to at least four different things. Risk can refer to whether the person will or will not commit a future crime of any kind. Alternatively, dangerousness can be weighed in terms of the type of crime with an emphasis upon the amount of harm to the victim brought about by the criminal act. The number of victims placed in harm's way by a crime or by successive crimes could be deemed critical. Finally, others might focus on the response of the criminal to rehabilitation efforts that seek to change his criminal ways. It seems unlikely that the same risk figure would be assigned to these four parameters of criminal conduct when considering degree of dangerousness for a given individual. How dangerous a person may appear to be depends upon what risk you choose to examine.

The best that our research efforts could accomplish was to separate these four parameters of criminal risk and to study them independently in an effort to validate the dangerousness model. For the most part, we have concentrated upon differences in harm to the victim implicit in the type of crime committed. This was investigated in two ways. The differential severity of varying types of crime was related to the dangerousness of the criminal, and those results will be reported in this chapter. Differences in the harm extended to the victim within the same type of crime by men differing in dangerousness will be covered in the chapter to follow. The risk of criminal recidivism and harm to successive victims along with incorrigibility in response to efforts to modify criminal conduct will be treated as correlates of dangerousness in chapters that follow.

Dangerousness of Violent and Nonviolent Criminals

The most basic test of the theoretical model under programmatic investigation is one in which the dangerousness of violent criminals is compared to that found in nonviolent offenders. Crimes that involve physical harm to the victims, or at least threaten such harm, are generally agreed to be the more serious crimes as far as victim impact is concerned and should have been perpetrated by more dangerous men. The more common violent crimes include murder, manslaughter, rape, child molestation, incest, assault, battery, robbery, terroristic threat, arson (that threatens or causes injury), and vehicular homicide. Other sexual offenses that do not involve physical contact with the victim such as exhibitionism, voyeurism, and telephone obscenity, although rarely represented in our samples, are included as violent based upon possible psychological impact upon the victim. Nonviolent criminals would be expected to fall lower on the dangerousness dimension, and their so-called property crimes involve burglary, theft (of various types), larceny, fraud, criminal trespass, and drug offenses. To qualify as a nonviolent criminal in our investigations would further require that the individual's criminal history include no record of violent offenses. The opposite requirement was not introduced for violent criminals; while they were identified as violent by their most recent crime of record, they may or may not have been convicted of previous nonviolent crimes. To the best we could determine from official criminal history, then, violent criminals had been convicted of at least one violent act, and nonviolent criminals had never been convicted of a violent crime.

Heilbrun (1979) reported the contingency between each of the antisociality/cognitive-impairment patterns shown by a sample of 76 male prisoners and the violent or nonviolent character of their offenses. This initial study of criminal dangerousness did not take advantage of the continuous score provided by a dangerousness index that soon was to become a standard part of our methodology. Rather, the relationships between patterns of antisociality and cognitive status, on the one hand, and violent/nonviolent criminality, on the other, were explored by categorical procedures. The Pd-So and IQ scores for the 76 prisoners were cut at their sample medians, and the men were assigned to one of the four resulting combinations. The theoretically most dangerous group were those who presented high antisociality and low IQ scores, and it was this subset of men who were expected to have been more inclined to violent crime.

The ratios of violent to nonviolent criminals in each antisociality/IQ grouping were compared by nonparametric statistical analysis. The 17 violent: 2 nonviolent ratio (89% violent) of the most dangerous group differed significantly from the remaining ratios provided by prisoners who qualified as low antisocial-high IQ (15 violent: 7 nonviolent, 68% violent), high antisocial-high IQ (10 violent: 9 nonviolent, 53% violent), and low antisocial-low IQ (8 violent: 8 nonviolent, 50% violent). The proportional differences among these groups varied reliably ($p<.05$). Although the theoretically dangerous combination of high antisociality and low intelligence was associated with the highest rate of criminal violence, the hypothetical ordering of the four prisoner groups was not in evidence. The low antisociality-high intelligence criminal group, which would be the least dangerous according to the model, presented the second highest ratio of violent to nonviolent crime. In this initial study, the dangerousness model proved to be a more definitive postdictor of who would be a violent criminal that who would not.

The small sample size of the 1979 study encouraged another comparison of dangerousness for men committing violent crimes and less harmful nonviolent crimes for purposes of this book. A far larger sample of parole cases had collected by 1994, including over 20 years of prisoners who had been sent for parole assessment and for whom personality tests were available. The more recent nature of this follow-up analysis gave me the opportunity to measure dangerousness by the quantitative index score. Some 504 violent prisoners provided a mean index score of 2543.89 which is to be compared with a mean score of 2327.29 for 101 nonviolent criminals. The violent criminal does appear more dangerous than his nonviolent counterpart ($p<.001$) as the model requires.

A more refined analysis of this replication sample, to be reported a few pages ahead, will offer some insight into why the difference in mean dangerousness scores for violent and nonviolent offenders in general is not even more dramatic. Criminal violence covers a broad span of offenses that are committed by men who vary widely in dangerousness. The more detailed analysis of violent criminals will make this point emphatically and introduce some new dangerousness figures that place the comparison with nonviolent criminals in clearer perspective.

Dangerousness in Criminals at Varying Levels of Violence Severity

The dangerousness model under investigation found empirical support at the most basic level of discrimination between violent and nonviolent criminals in the two studies already reported, although this kind of gross comparison did not bring striking differences. A reasonable next step in the between-crime comparison would be to increase the precision of discrimination required to validate the dangerousness model. Would the model be capable of more fine-tuned distinctions? This was undertaken in a study reported by Heilbrun (1990a) in which the dangerousness index scores of violent criminals only were compared after being broken down by crime severity levels. The question became whether the index could go beyond gross discrimination between more dangerous violent criminals and less dangerous nonviolent criminals to the more refined discrimination between types of violent criminals.

The effort to establish whether the dangerousness index can make a more precise discrimination between types of violent offenders requires some basis for ordering violence by severity. The actual harm to the victim involved in the various forms of criminal violence represents an obvious place to start in establishing the dangerousness of the behavior. For example, most would agree that physical assault involves greater actual harm to the victim than terroristic threat and that murder maximizes harm to a victim, exceeding the damaging effects of physical assault.

Considering the amount of physical harm to victims goes a long way in dimensionalizing the severity of crimes, but it is not the only factor that must be considered. Intentionality plays a role. Murder as an intentional killing is treated much more seriously in the courts than manslaughter or vehicular homicide in which the victim is just as dead but the acts are lacking in premeditation. While it could be argued that murder and manslaughter are equally dangerous as far as the fate of the victim is concerned, dangerousness of the perpetrator clearly differs. The willingness to kill marks the murderer as a greater risk to victims than unintended killing.

Yet another factor influencing the severity of violent crimes is the risk that criminal action directed toward other people may take a more serious turn and erupt into violence. Robbery is considered to be a serious violent crime even though no physical harm may be involved, because the victim is threatened with serious physical injury. Rape also qualifies as a serious violent crime not only because of the sexual aggression itself but because forced sexual contact and victim resistance that are frequently involved increase the chances that physical harm will escalate.

Finally, in what could be a far-longer list of factors to be considered in determining the relative severity of violent crimes, the psychological repercussions for the victim of violent conduct should not be ignored. Rape again offers a clear example of how sexual violence can be far more harmful to the victim than the bodily damage caused by the crime. The emotional anguish caused by the sexual aggression itself and the psychological distress that commonly follows victimization make rape a more harmful form of violence. The hierarchy of severity among violent crimes, key to the study that will be reported next, takes all of these factors into consideration -- actual physical harm to the victim, potential physical harm, intentionality of the criminal act, and psychological impact upon the victim.

Taking a severity-level approach to ordering crimes of a violent nature is not meant to imply that differences in dangerousness within specific types of violent crime are not to be assumed. All rapes are not equally devastating to the victims as far as physical harm and psychological repercussions are concerned. Even though all murders involve the death of a victim, some are conducted in a more brutal and inhumane fashion than others; that is one reason why the death penalty is retained as a punishment choice. These within-crime variations in dangerous conduct are overlooked when crimes are treated categorically as in the study to be described next. They were not ignored in our program of research, however.

The comparison between various types of violent criminals on the dangerousness index (Heilbrun, 1990a) involved three severity categories; the criminal's assignment to a given category was dependent upon the most serious display of criminal violence appearing in his conviction record. The table of crime levels graded by severity employed by the Georgia Board of Pardons and Paroles, and modeled after the procedure used by the Federal Parole Commission, served as the basis for ordering violent crimes. The seven crime-severity levels within the table are used by the Parole Board to partially determine how long prisoners must remain in prison. All types of crime bringing less than a life sentence in the Georgia judicial system are included. Murder, which brings either a mandatory life sentence or death penalty, is not found on the table, but I added this crime to the study as representing the most severe level of criminal violence in keeping with these maximum sentences and commonsense.

Severity levels I and II within the Parole Board table are comprised of only nonviolent crimes. Level III introduces involuntary manslaughter at the lowest level of severity for a violent crime. Rape and armed robbery appear at the highest severity level VII. Other violent crimes fall between levels III and VII. The following crime groupings respected the order imposed by the table and completed the tri-level separation of violent offenses by presumed dangerousness of the criminal. Murder represented high severity violence; robbery and rape were considered intermediate in severity; and assault, manslaughter, and child molestation qualified as violent crimes of low severity. The results required to support the theoretical model are clear; as the severity of violence increases, the dangerousness of the criminal should be greater. Subjects for this study were male criminals drawn randomly from parole-assessment files except for requiring that their histories of crime include one of the relevant violent offenses. If more than one of these violent crimes had been committed by a subject, he was assigned to the more severe category given such a distinction.

Table 1 presents the mean dangerousness scores for criminals in the three violence categories. Inspection of the table shows the predicted order of index scores, and statistical analysis revealed significant ($p<.01$) variation among the means. Validation of the dangerous model, then, progressed with this result from gross discrimination between violent and nonviolent criminals to what should be a more demanding discrimination between categories of violent criminals ordered by severity of their violence.

The large backlog of prisoners seen for parole assessment and used for follow-up comparison of violent and nonviolent criminals reported earlier in this chapter can serve us well at this point as well. This ever-expanding sample will not only allow me to repeat the within-violence analysis of dangerousness with increased numbers of criminals, but it also will make it possible to introduce a more diverse

Table 1:Dangerousness Index Scores for Criminals Convicted of Violent Crimes at Varying Severity Levels

High-Severity Violence[a]		Intermediate-Severity Violence[b]		Low-Severity Violence[c]	
N	M	N	M	N	M
77	2660.99	104	2504.07	94	2351.93

[a] Murder

[b] Robbery, rape

[c] Assault, manslaughter, child molestation

set of violent crimes into the comparisons. Adding new violent offenses required some minor shuffling of crimes encompassed by the three severity categories, always subject to the ordering of violence severity within the Parole Board table. Footnotes to forthcoming Table 2 provide the reconstituted violence-severity categories. A final advantage to the follow-up analysis was the inclusion of a nonviolent comparison group that was missing in the 1990 study. This will cast further light on the dangerousness of violent criminals relative to nonviolent that I promised when this gross discrimination was being discussed a few pages back.

Table 2 offers average index scores for men falling in the three revised violence-severity categories and for male nonviolent criminals. Comparison of the four dangerousness means revealed significant variation among them ($p<.001$), and examination of the mean values disclosed the same ordering of violence severity as in the original 1990 study. It seems safe to conclude that the dangerousness model can distinguish appropriately between violent men with respect to dangerousness and the risk of varying degrees of harm to the victims of their crimes.

Inspection of Table 2 also portrays a similarity in index-score averages between men committing low-severity violence and nonviolent criminals. The comparable (actually, identical) dangerousness scores for these groups help to explain why the most general comparisons between violent and nonviolent criminals did not provide more robust differences. As you include more of the violent men from the least severe category in this kind of general comparison, it becomes increasingly difficult to distinguish between the dangerousness of violent and nonviolent men.

Perhaps some might challenge, crime-severity tables notwithstanding, the relatively low dangerousness scores for criminals who show such disregard for social morality in general and victim wellbeing in particular as would be represented in child molestation, terroristic threat, and passive (noncontact) sex crimes. At least, it could be argued, these crimes involving low-severity violence seem more conducive to victim harm than do nonviolent property crimes and dangerousness scores should reflect this.

Such an argument does not pose a problem for the dangerousness model, however. In theory, the dangerous offender is likely to engage in crimes because of his antisociality and to become violent with a victim for one of two reasons. Impaired cognition may result in

Table 2: Dangerousness Index Scores for Men Falling in Three Violence-Severity Categories and for Male Nonviolent Criminals

High-Severity Violence[a]		Intermediate-Severity Violence[b]		Low-Severity Violence[c]		Nonviolent	
N	M	N	M	N	M	N	M
100	2746.63	301	2528.93	103	2327.29	101	2327.29

[a] Murder

[b] Robbery, rape, sodomy, assault, battery, cruelty to children

[c] Manslaughter, child molestation, peeping Tom, exhibitionism, obscene phone calls, terroristic threat

poorly-orchestrated crimes that introduce risk for the victim that might otherwise be avoided by more astute criminals. In addition, cognitive limitations may allow criminal transactions with the victim to deteriorate into violence. The men responsible for committing violence in the least-severe category did not engage in crimes involving close interpersonal contact for the most part, so situationally-induced violence is less of a risk. Even when children are the victims of adult sexual aggression and there is contact between the criminal and his target, fewer transactional confrontations would be expected because of age or status differences between criminal and victim in child molestation or incest. Criminals in the least-severe category kill without intent, prey upon children, passively follow the dictates of their perverse sexual motives, and issue verbal threats to qualify as violent. They provide a poor fit to the dangerous prototype described by the model.

There is a second rationale for the overlap in dangerousness scores between men who commit violent crimes and those whose criminal record includes only nonviolent offenses. This explanation has less to do with why some violent offenders present low dangerousness scores and more to do with why some nonviolent criminals appear to be highly dangerous by score. So that I will not appear to be unduly defensive about limitations of the dangerousness model, I will accompany the proposal by a small piece of prospective data from a study to be reported in full several chapters ahead. I would propose that in any sample of men who have been convicted of only nonviolent crimes at a given point in time there will be some more dangerous criminals whose violence lies ahead. For whatever reason, their risk-provoking combination of antisociality and impaired cognition will not have as yet culminated in a violent criminal episode or at least one so blatant as to have been made a matter of record.

In order to prove the thesis of yet-undemonstrated violence for highly dangerous men, it would be necessary to track nonviolent criminals to establish future criminal patterns. A sample of 52 nonviolent criminals was followed for up to 20 years past the time their dangerousness index was established and they were placed on parole. Thirteen of these men (25%) remained free of further crime; their dangerousness score mean was 2293.15. A larger number ($\underline{N}$=30, 58%) committed one or more nonviolent offenses during the tracking period, and their average dangerousness was somewhat higher ($\underline{M}$=2457.63). The critical group for purpose of this discussion included the nine men (17%) who eventually engaged in criminal violence. These men showed an extremely high dangerousness mean of 2994.67. The values of these three means and their significant variation ($p<.01$) support the thesis that high dangerousness in nonviolent offenders, a seeming error of measurement, signals risk of future violence.

Dangerousness in Criminals Committing Sexual Offenses Involving Physical Contact with the Victim

This analysis narrowed the scope of between-crime comparison even more as the dangerousness of only violent sex-offenders was considered with the added stipulation that physical contact occurred between the criminal and the victim. A more detailed analysis of dangerousness restricted exclusively to different types of sex-offenders who make physical contact with their victims will provide a more focused look at the ability of the index and the theoretical model to discriminate between types of violent criminals. This will represent a more rigorous test of the model's power since passive sex-offenders (voyeurs, exhibitionists, obscene telephone callers) will not be included to potentially reduce the dangerousness scores of men committing low-severity violence. A new sample of sex-offenders was considered for this analysis, so this more focused analysis also represented a replication of sorts.

The efforts of two researchers working in the dangerousness research program (Hollmann, 1990; Wasieleski, 1990) made available 278 male sex-offenders and allowed this more finely-tuned examination of relative dangerousness for types of sex criminals. Their data also made possible a host of additional analyses that shall be reported later in the book. The Hollmann-Wasieleski sample included men whose crime(s) included rape, sometimes coupled with sodomy; child molestation; and incest. Both rape and incest as crimes proved to be exclusively heterosexual in their samples, whereas the child molestation group included a predominance (70%) of men who victimized female children.

This analysis of sex-offenders derives its validational status from the crime-severity table that played a prominent role in the comparisons of violent crime categories that I have reported. Men found guilty of incest, in almost every case a father sexually abusing his daughter, were added as a new comparison group. Incest cases fall at the same severity level as child molestation. Accordingly, correspondence of dangerousness scores with the crime-severity table would require that the severity-level VII rapists be found more dangerous than the level V child sex-offenders of either type. Child molesters and men committing incest should present similar dangerousness scores.

Table 3 presents the average dangerousness scores for the three sex-crime groups from the new sample. Statistical analysis confirmed the significant differences among these mean scores ($p<.001$). As is evident from inspection, the variation in index scores was largely a matter of the very high dangerousness of the rapists (M=2844.93) and the relatively low scores of child molesters (M=2333.97) and men committing incest (M=2377.57). The rapists were more dangerous than either child-victimizing group ($ps<.001$), and the latter groups presented much the same average scores on the index. Differentiating more dangerous rapists from both child-victim groups supports the validity of the dangerousness index as does the almost-identical low dangerousness scores for child molesters and perpetrators of incest.

There is replication to a point in finding that aggressive rapists are more dangerous than men who choose children as their sexual victims, since this was implicit in the previous severity-level studies. There is also an ominous note struck by these findings, at least in theory. Dangerous men who rape are the least capable of formulating criminal acts that will circumvent complications and the least capable of dealing with complications involving the victim that may arise. However, these are the very men who target adults who are likely to offer some degree of resistance to their sexual aggression. Rapists, who are least prepared to contend with transactional complications, are those who invite them by the nature of their sex-offenses.

Table 3:   Dangerousness Index Scores of Rapists, Child Molesters and Men Committing Incest

Rape		Child Molestation		Incest	
N	M	N	M	N	M
77	2844.93	161	2333.97	47	2377.57

CHAPTER 4

Validation of the Dangerousness Model Based Upon Within-Crime Comparisons

The strategy for substantiating the dangerousness model described to this point has involved the most obvious validity criterion -- degree of harm to the victim associated with the most serious type of crime committed by the prisoner. As long as dangerousness is defined in terms of the risk of harming a victim through criminal behavior, it makes sense to examine the type of past criminal activities in order to assess current risk. It is not the only criterion, of course, and it does involve postdiction rather than prediction into the future, but it is a reasonable place to start.

Using discrimination between criminal types as the validating procedure provided incremental challenges to the dangerousness model when increasing precision was required for a succession of distinctions called for by the model. We began with the requirement that the index score distinguish only between men who have committed a violent crime and those whose crimes to date have been nonviolent -- differentiating criminals who fall at the opposite ends of the dangerousness dimension. The requirement that violent men obtain higher scores was satisfied. Following this, analysis was directed at only violent criminals. The question became whether the index could discriminate between categories of violence in an order predicated upon a table of severity. Violent men who have the most physically and psychologically damaging impact upon the victim through act or threat should prove to be more dangerous than men whose violence is deemed less harmful. Criminals who lacked intent in their commission of violence would be considered less of a future risk to new victims.

Validation at this more demanding level was successful as categories of violent crime from most to least severe fell into the prescribed order of criminal dangerousness. Subsequently, a new analysis narrowed the focus to violent sex-criminals who initiate physical contact with their victims, and the specifications of the crime-severity table were again satisfied by the dangerousness model. Men who commit the more serious crime of rape proved especially dangerous relative to men who molest children, a less serious offense. On the other hand it made no difference whether the child victims were not family members (molestation) or were (incest); these crimes of equal severity were associated with equal dangerousness of the perpetrators.

The present chapter will continue to examine index validation by past crime but at an even more demanding level. Three violent crimes, representing widely-separate levels of criminal severity, will be exposed independently to within-crime analysis. The purpose of this approach was to determine whether the dangerousness index can make appropriate discriminations between men who have been convicted of the same crime. Each type of violence will be evaluated case by case in terms of the specific circumstances and conduct associated with the crimes. Two research questions required answers. Would it be possible to distinguish between men who had been convicted of the same violent crime but committed the acts in more or less brutal ways? The second question concerned whether this within-crime discrimination in dangerousness could be achieved at both extremes of violence severity. That is, can discrimination be achieved when all of the men had been responsible for the most severe form of violence (murder) or, in the opposite case, when all of the offenders had engaged in what is considered one of the least severe forms of violence (child molestation). Rape, as an intermediate-severity violent crime, was included in the within-crime analyses for sake of completeness, although the volatile nature of this form of sexual aggression made the analysis interesting in its own right.

Within-Crime Analysis of Child Molestation

It may be remembered that the child-molestation group within the Hollmann-Wasieleski sample included men who solicited heterosexual victims (70%) as well as homosexual sex-offenders. No separate analysis of these child molesters by gender of the victim was initially contemplated, since the sampling was essentially random for these and the remaining sex-offender groups that they collected. It was assumed from the case selection procedures that they had drawn a representative sample of child molesters as far as sexual orientation was concerned, and generalization from the sample to a broader population of sex-offenders victimizing children was not a problem. However, the possibility remained that the heterosexual or homosexual nature of molestation might prove useful as a validating distinction for the dangerousness model.

Anticipating a difference between heterosexual and homosexual molesters is in large measure based upon clinical impression and results of various sex-offender surveys. West (1969) describes the typical child molester, whether heterosexually or homosexually oriented (or both), as timorous, inhibited, and gentle in soliciting sexual contact with children. He further emphasizes the nonviolent nature of the typical child sexual offense, by which he alluded to the usual absence of physical injury. However, he did make reference to a systematic study of sex-offenders by the Institute for Sex Research at Indiana University that brought the child-molesting prototype into clearer perspective (Gebhard, 1965). The Institute survey reported that in the case of 200 men committing acts of child molestation against boys, not one instance of serious physical violence was noted. The same survey painted a contrasting picture for heterosexual child molesters whose ranks included some who physically assaulted their girl victims and a few who engaged in even more serious violence. Based upon this evidence, heterosexual child offenders would be expected to be more dangerous than homosexual offenders in order to achieve within-crime validation of the model.

Dangerousness scores, involving an antisociality metric based upon file ratings, had been assigned to child molesters in the more inclusive Hollmann-Wasieleski sample of sex criminals initially considered in the previous chapter. These scores also served as the basis for comparing heterosexual and homosexual child molesters in the present analysis. The mean index score of the 138 heterosexual child molesters ($\underline{M}$=2457.13) was far above the average score for the 23 homosexual molesters ($\underline{M}$=1945.04). The difference was quite reliable (p<.001) and in line with expectations from clinical and survey observations; the male child molester who targets girls is more dangerous in terms of the model than the homosexual offender.

The very low level of dangerousness implicit in the average score obtained by homosexual molesters puts their risk far below that of any other contact sex-offender group as Table 3 in the preceding chapter makes clear. The clinical evidence of very low risk for physical violence observed in this type of offender's reported sexual contact with boys also would follow from the sub-2000 index score, a rare finding for criminal types in our research. Heterosexual child molesters, reportedly more likely to harm their female victims, obtained a dangerousness score ($\underline{M}$=2457.13) that was still well below that of the adult rapist ($\underline{M}$=2844.93) reported in the earlier table but by less of a margin than the original child-molester group.

The greater potential for harm presented by heterosexual child molesters, relative to their homosexual counterparts, is reflected not only in their higher index scores but also in an additional correlate of dangerousness abstracted from criminal files by Hollmann and Wasieleski. Ratings of intoxication from either alcohol or drugs during the sex-offender's crime were made. This variable will be considered at greater length in the next chapter, but it serves a theoretical purpose to touch upon intoxication effects now.

Dangerousness in the model under investigation derives in part from deficits in self-control and in other higher-order cognitive functions. These deficiencies, according to theory, allow poorly-conceived criminal behavior to evolve that place others at more serious risk or for the criminal transaction to otherwise deteriorate into more dangerous circumstances for the victim. What if the criminal's continuing deficits in cognition are coupled with episodic debilitating effects of intoxication at the time a crime is anticipated or transacted? The compromise of effective thought and action from the combination should bring even more poorly conceived criminality and increase the risk of more harmful violent transactions with the victim. If the child molester (or any other criminal who confronts his victim) was not particularly dangerous before, according to the model, the effects of intoxication should enhance dangerousness beyond that evident in the index score.

The intoxication ratings for the child molesters in the Hollmann-Wasieleski sample were made on a 4-point scale. Based upon the reported circumstances of the crimes, the two investigators rated the criminal as not at all, mildly, moderately, or greatly intoxicated as a result of alcohol or drugs at the time he molested his victim. Scores from 0 to 3 were assigned as rated intoxication increased. Homosexual child molesters provided an average intoxication level of .57, reliably less ($\underline{p}$<.05) than the 1.04 figure found for the heterosexual molesters.

Closer examination of the men who molested girls by splitting them into dangerousness levels revealed that the difference in intoxication at the time of their offenses varied with dangerousness within their group as well. (This was not true for the homosexual child-molester group.) Those men who fell above the median dangerousness score for heterosexual molesters were more intoxicated when they sexually abused their girl victims ($\underline{M}$=1.22) than were their less dangerous counterparts who fell below the median ($\underline{M}$=.83, $\underline{p}$<.05).

Considered overall, we can see a progressive increment in intoxication during the crime as the dangerousness of the child molester increases. Homosexual molesters, almost benign by sex-offender standards of scored dangerousness, show little inclination to act while intoxicated. There is little reason to expect escalation of violence because of impaired cognitive functions. Heterosexual molesters are generally more dangerous by model specifications; even the less dangerous among them present greater risk for the victim, because they act while slightly more intoxicated than the homosexually inclined. It is the more dangerous heterosexual molesters, as defined by index score, that are a special concern regarding risk to the children they victimize. Not only are they dangerous to begin with, but they molest children at a level of intoxication that was rated mild to moderate on average. Dangerous behavior on the part of riskier heterosexual molesters involves two sources of threat to the girl. Victim risk results from both the limitations in value development and cognition that have occupied our attention to this point and the inclination to act while intoxicated so that they have even less judgment and self-control than usual.

Within-Crime Analysis of Rape

A sample of 142 male rapists was collected from Parole Board central files in order to consider the dangerousness of the criminal as it relates to degree of harm to the rape victim. One criterion of harm involved ratings of physical brutality of the act as judged from the crime report included in the rapist's case file. These ratings were made on a 5-point scale extending from no discernible physical harm (score=0) to great physical harm (score=4). The information available regarding the crime made it possible to also rate a second parameter of harm to the victim. How much psychological distress did the woman experience during the rape? These ratings were recorded on the same 5-point scale as was used for physical brutality with the range extending from no discernible psychological distress (score=0) to great psychological distress (score=4). This second set of ratings was not intended to reflect the lingering distress of some female victims months or even years after being raped. Long-term information on the effects of rape was not available to us. Rather, psychological distress embraced the emotional responses of the victim to intimidation and threat by the rapist and to the repugnant sexual experience. Harm, then, should be understood to mean the amount of physical hurt and psychological distress suffered by the rape victim during the crime.

The question might be raised as to whether physical brutality involved in the rape and the psychological distress induced in the victim might not be so highly related as to be redundant as indicators of harm -- that psychological distress derives for the most part from actual physical harm. A correlation of .42 was found when the two sets of ratings were correlated. While this figure confirms some degree of relationship, the low 18% common variance suggests enough independent contribution to combine the two ratings for each case of rape. The sum of the ratings, designating the overall physical and psychological harm to the victim, could range from 0 to 8. The entire range was represented in the sample of rape cases.

A check on the authenticity of the ratings of harm to the victim was available by determining whether the punishment accorded to the rapist for his crime fell in line with this summary indicator of harm. There are other factors that may influence the severity of punishment following conviction, but victim impact should certainly rank high among sentencing considerations. (It was possible to show that whether the rapist was a recidivist or not had no significant bearing upon his punishment, so at least that source of influence could be eliminated.) The cases of rape within the sample were split into three groups as the best way to accommodate the variation in sentencing. The predominant sentence for rape was 20 years ($\underline{N}$=58), and this was defined as intermediate punishment. Twenty-seven men were punished severely (>20 years), with 24 receiving life terms. Sentences from 5 to 18 years were being served by the 57 men accorded the least severe punishment. Statistical comparison of the ratings of victim harm for cases receiving these three levels of punishment revealed significant differences ($\underline{p}$<.01) that fell in the predicted order. Men who had been given the stiffest sentences had been the most brutal to their victims during the rape ($\underline{M}$=6.37); intermediate sentences were associated with intermediate harm ($\underline{M}$=5.00); and the men who were least severely punished were the least brutal ($\underline{M}$=4.16). The agreement between the rated brutality of sexual aggression and severity of punishment lends confidence to the ratings.

The issue of whether rapist brutality is related to his dangerousness index score can now be addressed. By cutting the distribution of brutality ratings at its median, the sample of rapists was separated into those who had been excessively brutal to their victims in the course of their sexual aggression (ratings of 6-8) and those who were less harmful (ratings of 0-5). The more brutal rapists ($\underline{N}$=70) presented a dangerousness score of 2680.37. This was significantly higher ($\underline{p}$<.01) than was found for the 72 men who were less harmful to their victims and whose index mean was 2329.67. Again we find that within-crime analysis provides support for the dangerousness model.

For the sake of completeness, the triangulation of brutality ratings, severity of sentencing, and criminal dangerousness was completed by examining the relationship between sentence and the dangerousness of the rapist. This analysis is not independent of those previously reported but may prove of interest. Men whose crimes brought the most severe sentences (usually a life term) had index scores with a mean of 2766.15. In-between sentences of 20 years were extended to rapists with an index average of 2555.59, and the least-severe sentences of under 20 years were given to rapists whose index scores averaged 2318.10. These differences were found to be reliable ($\underline{p}$<.05). This analysis, like the previous one relating brutality of the rape to dangerousness of the rapist, is consistent with the validity of the theoretical model. It also strikes a reassuring note regarding the criminal justice system. Predictably more dangerous men tend to brutalize their victims during a rape, but they do receive the added punishment they deserve.

Within-Crime Analysis of Murder

At first consideration it might appear that murder as a criminal act of violence might not readily accommodate a split into acts that are more and less harmful to the victim. The fullest measure of harm might seem to be represented in the victim's loss of life that defines the crime. However, examination of the circumstances and treatment of the victim over a series of murders makes it clear that the victims are made to suffer physically and psychologically to far different degrees before they die and that intentional cruelty varies from one case to the next. In fact, state laws make allowance for different punishments depending upon aggravating circumstances surrounding the murder, and these aggravations include how brutally the victim is treated in the conduct of the crime. Georgia law, for example, stipulates that the death penalty can be imposed in the case of murder if at least 1 of 10 statutory aggravating circumstances was involved. Commission of a murder in an outrageously vile, horrible, or inhuman fashion represents one such aggravating circumstance.

The especially brutal treatment of the murder victim is not the only aggravating circumstance that points to the special dangerousness of the criminal receiving the death penalty. Other aggravating circumstances that might bring the death penalty in a murder trial also mark the criminal not only as an extraordinary risk to the particular victim of his crime but as a wide-ranging risk to others and to society's system of law that is supposed to protect innocent people from harm. Such additional aggravating circumstances (in Georgia) include a record of prior capital felony, murder during commission of another capital felony, knowingly risking the death of more than one person in a public place, murdering for pay, directing the commission of a murder, and several others involving the killing of judicial officers, lawyers, or peace officers while they are conducting their duties. The death penalty imposed for any of these circumstances would follow from the criminals' profound disregard for human life and the system of laws and values that are supposed to afford protection from wrongdoing in a civilized society. In other words, those who receive the death penalty in murder cases are very dangerous criminals no matter what the aggravating circumstance(s) might be.

A study comparing death-penalty murderers (DPM) and life-sentence murderers (LSM) was conducted to test whether the dangerousness model could differentiate appropriately between men who had been convicted of this most serious of all violent crimes (Heilbrun, 1990b). The sample of murderers included all men awaiting the death penalty in the Georgia prison system ($\underline{N}$=109) and a randomly-selected comparison group of life-term murderers ($\underline{N}$=134). The first analysis involved a comparison of these two groups with respect to dangerousness, with validity support for the model requiring a higher index score for the death-row inmates. Validation was achieved when the death-penalty murderers (DPM) received higher scores on the index (M=2658.50) than the life-sentence murderers (LSM) (M=2360.83), and a statistical test of the difference proved significant (p<.01).

This seems an especially appropriate place to reiterate one aspect of the quantification procedures that were followed in all of our studies involving the dangerousness index, since the average index score of the DPM group, the most dangerous of all criminals that we studied, may not seem as high as it should. The reader is reminded that the index scores are determined independently for each study as new samples are drawn. The mean dangerousness score of 2658.50 for the DPM group was obtained by applying the indexing procedures to murderers only. The critical feature of this score is that it is higher relative to the average score of the LSM group. The absolute value of either mean cannot be compared directly to the results obtained in another study, even to the average dangerousness score of another group of murderers. For example, the murderers reported in Table 1 (Chapter 3) obtained a dangerousness score slightly higher than the present death-row group even though none of these murderers was given a death penalty. They compare in dangerousness to the DPM group only because they were introduced into the quantification procedures with violent criminals committing far less harmful crimes.

One further effort to refine prediction was attempted in order to put the dangerousness model to its most strenuous test using within-crime discrimination as the methodology of choice. This involved selection of the most heinous murderers in the DPM group, those whose choice and treatment of their victims most radically breached the moral constraints of society, as the ultimate standard of criminal dangerousness. These 31 men received the death penalty for their crime, requiring that they had engaged in the most serious form of violence and had done so with aggravation. In addition, we confirmed that their victims had been women in violation of the moral constraint against male physical aggression toward a female. Ratings of cruelty involved in the killings allowed for further identification of those who were particularly cruel (i.e., above the median rating) in the way they ended the life of their female victims.

Table 4 presents the average dangerousness index scores for this

Table 4: Dangerousness of Convicted Murderers as a Function of Sentence, Cruelty of the Murder, and Victim Gender

Sentence	Cruel Murder of a Female Victim		Cruel Murder of a Male Victim		Murder of a Female or Male Victim Without Cruelty	
	N	M	N	M	N	M
Death Penalty	31	2902.45	22	2433.23	22	2490.09
Life Sentence	17	2400.06	26	2229.35	83	2393.99

particularly heinous group of death-row murderers along with the means for a variety of comparison groups in which sentence, victim gender, and degree of cruelty were combined in other ways. The men within the DPM group, who had killed a woman in an excessively cruel fashion, were singularly high on the index ($\underline{M}$=2902.45); all other groups of murderers were similar to each other ($\underline{M}$=2229.35-2490.09) and relatively low on these scores. The combined mean of 2386.93 for all comparison groups lumped together fell well below the index score for the subset of DPM convicts selected for their especially heinous criminal behavior ($\underline{p}$<.001).

It can be noted that the index scores for the especially dangerous subset of murderers reported in Table 4 are also elevated substantially above those for the 44 death-penalty murderers whose crimes either lacked excessive cruelty or did not target a female victim ($\underline{M}$=2461.66). This significant difference ($\underline{p}$<.01) adds to the lengthy record of increasingly more difficult discriminations between criminals that have been possible using the dangerousness index. Predicted between-crime differences were found between criminals committing crimes that were violent or nonviolent or that fell at three levels of severity considering violent crimes alone. Reducing the focus of analysis to only violent sex-offenses involving contact with the victim, the index revealed the predicted pattern of scores based upon severity tables. Within-crime analysis revealed appropriate differences in dangerousness within sex-offender groups associated with low-severity violence (child molestation) or violence of intermediate severity (rape). The study just described continued the trend of valid within-crime discrimination to the high-severity crime of murder. Now, differentiation has been carried to a new extreme in which the worst of violent offenders have been distinguished from the rest of the men receiving the death penalty for their egregious murders -- discrimination within a single severity level of a single violent crime.

CHAPTER 5

Validation of the Dangerousness Model Based Upon Criteria of Continuing Risk

To this point validation of the proposed dangerousness model has depended upon a singular type of evidence--the criminal's most serious offense. This criterion represents a reasonable point of departure for establishing the validity and power of the dangerousness index. The only assumptions required are that an individual's risk for harming others by some criminal act and the extent of that harm to the victim can be gauged by the individual's past behavior -- his criminal history. That current and future responses are correlated with past conduct of the individual is axiomatic to the understanding and prediction of human behavior. The evidence garnered from these studies of past offenses supported model validity at every level of specificity tested. Successive validation extended all the way from between violent and nonviolent criminals to precise differentiation within a group of death-row murderers by the degree of depravity characterizing their crimes.

There are several other sources of validation for the dangerousness model besides seriousness of past crime, although alternative criteria were less thoroughly considered because of logistical constraints upon my research program. These will be covered in this chapter and the next. Perhaps the most convenient way to think about the additional criteria of model validity is to consider them as either crime-related or model-related. Those that are crime-related readily tie into the issue of victim harm and would be relevant to any consideration of dangerousness. These criteria, to be examined in this chapter, will have more to do with continuity of criminal activity -- dangerousness from the perspective of incorrigibility rather than worst crime. How prone is the offender to criminal recidivism? How responsive is the prisoner to rehabilitation opportunities within the prison system? How prepared is the criminal to meet the requirements of community living after he is paroled from prison? Dangerousness would be implied by repeated criminal activity as recidivism confirms a sustained risk of harming a succession of victims. Unresponsiveness to rehabilitation in prison portends further crimes and a continued risk to future victims. Ability to remain out of trouble in the community and to conform to parole conditions after release from prison offers another barometer of sustained risk of harming new victims. Parole failure signals a continuing problem in conforming to rules of conduct.

The second kind of evidence, to be considered in the next chapter, can be thought of as validating only because of the assumptions of my dangerousness model. This evidence will address theoretical questions rather than the practical issues of criminal behavior and response to criminal justice efforts to reshape criminality. One paramount question will concern us. Is criminal dangerousness, as indicated by index score, associated with other psychological attributes and demographic characteristics that add to the risk of harm to crime victims? If so, the power of the theoretical model would be enhanced.

Three crime-related criteria of dangerousness will be considered in this chapter, each offering a different time perspective with regard to crime, imprisonment, and participation in our research. Recidivism will be defined in terms of whether the most recent (index) crime prior to serving as a subject while in prison represents a first offense or whether the criminal has been convicted of a felony on one or more prior occasions. Prison conduct will focus upon the adjustment of the criminal to incarceration that follows conviction for the most recent crime. Parole outcome considers the results of the criminal's parole behavior after he has served his allotted time in prison following the index crime. In every case, who should be at higher risk of continuing harm to victims of crime seems clear. Criminal recidivism, disruptive and violent prison adjustment, and poorer parole outcome would be expected for more dangerous criminals as identified by the theoretical model.

Criminal Recidivism and Parole Outcome as Criteria of Dangerousness

The two criteria of dangerousness bearing upon continuity of risk in the community will be considered together in the present section. This grouping was called for, since there is a suggestion of relationship, even overlap, in these criteria; parole failure is sometimes the result of criminal recidivism by the parolee. The manner in which I define recidivism for purpose of testing the dangerousness model helps to disentangle these criteria of continuing risk, yet concern about their independence is best satisfied by evidence. Accordingly, I will consider criminal recidivism and parole outcome in a joint analysis later in this section.

Parole outcome. Heilbrun and Heilbrun (1985) were the first to relate model-defined dangerousness of the criminal to parole outcome. In that study parole status of 144 felons was rated along a 9-point scale starting with $0 =$ no parole violation, into points 1 and 2 (technical violations), to point $3 =$ commission of a nonviolent crime. Points 4-8 represented five levels of severity for a violent crime. This scale of parole outcome, when examined after the data had been collected, seemed to lack sensitivity, since the ratings were heavily skewed toward the low end. Very few violent crimes were committed during the average period of three years that the criminals were tracked on parole, so points higher on the scale were of little value. Nevertheless, the high antisocial-low IQ men in the parole sample, determined by median splits on the two distributions, did demonstrate poorer adjustment on parole ($\underline{M}$=1.06, $\underline{N}$=31) than the remaining criminals combined ($\underline{M}$=.50, $\underline{N}$=113). The difference proved reliable ($\underline{p}$<.05).

These results do support the conclusion that dangerous men, as defined by the model, continue to demonstrate less inclination to conform to rules of conduct after they are released on parole into the community. The absolute value of their rated adjustment to parole does suggest that the high antisocial-low IQ group of criminals had substantial difficulties despite appearances to the contrary fostered by a 9-point rating scale. Their score of 1.06 indicates that on average the more dangerous group of parolees demonstrated the equivalent of a technical violation of parole conditions, often enough to return the man to prison as a failed case.

Criminal recidivism and parole outcome. The Hollmann (1990) and Wasieleski (1990) samples of sex-offenders that proved so valuable in between-crime and within-crime analyses of sex-offenders reported previously also offered me the opportunity to consider criminal recidivism and parole outcome as independent criteria of dangerousness.

The evidence relating to each criterion was abstracted from different points in the sex-offender's history so that the criminal recidivism could not have served as the basis for parole failure. Recidivism, as considered here, refers to whether the prisoner was a repeat sex-offender at the time of conviction for the index crime and incarceration. Parole outcome describes what happens to the same criminal after he completes this incarceration and leaves prison as a recidivist or first offender. Both Hollmann and Wasieleski used information that was available at the time of incarceration to determine the dangerousness index score. This means, then, that relating dangerousness to recidivism as a sex-offender represents a postdiction, but that the relation of dangerousness to parole outcome is a true prediction.

Parole outcome ratings for the Hollmann-Wasieleski sex-offenders were obtained on a different scale than that used in the Heilbrun and Heilbrun (1985) study. Less emphasis was placed on the specific type of criminal offense that might occur while the criminal was on parole, which did not prove to be particularly helpful, and more attention was given to the shades of adjustment to parole conditions. The 5-point parole-outcome scale included "discharged from parole" as the clearest evidence of favorable outcome, since this indicated that the parolee had satisfied his terms of parole well enough to gain his freedom. "On parole without problems" was the next best outcome; the man was continuing to meet all demands of social reentry. The next point, "on parole with problems," reflected a halting adjustment but as yet no return to prison. The failure extremes included "technical violation of parole" and "conviction for a new crime," both resulting in a return to prison. The first two rating points, representing problem-free adjustment, were considered successful parole outcome, whereas the latter three points were designated an unsuccessful adjustment to parole. The three major contact sex-offender groups were represented in the Hollmann and Wasieleski samples -- men who raped, molested children, or entered into incestuous acts with their daughters. These categories were retained in order to determine whether the dangerousness model would be validated on the two criteria of continuing risk across all types of contact sex-offenders.

Table 5 presents the mean dangerousness index scores for 273 convicted sex-offenders broken down by type of offense, recidivism as a sex offender, and success or failure on parole. Recidivists in each of the sex-offender groups emerged as more dangerous than the men who were incarcerated for their first sex-offense (p<.01). Put more in terms

Table 5: Recidivism of Sex-offenders, Success on Parole, and Dangerousness

	Type of Sex Offense					
	Rape		Child Molestation		Incest	
Criterion of Dangerousness	N	M	N	M	N	M
Recidivism						
Recidivist	11	3193.27	47	2650.04	10	2608.60
Nonrecidivist	60	2781.07	107	2314.79	37	2315.14
Parole Outcome						
Successful	32	2632.97	116	2311.57	38	2304.63
Unsuccessful	33	2939.88	45	2790.11	9	2685.56

Note: Discrepancies in numbers for the sex-offender groups between the two criterion analyses resulted from occasional gaps in information within the files.

of the dangerousness model, men who had been convicted of harming more victims through sexual aggressiveness were shown to be more dangerous by the index than men who had restricted their sexual aggression to one victim (at least of record). These results qualify as validating evidence, especially as the recidivism difference was replicated across each type of sex-offense.

When this same sample of sex-offenders was redistributed by successful/unsuccessful parole outcome, the results were quite similar. Men displaying problems on parole or who had already violated their parole and were returned to prison presented higher dangerousness scores ($p<.01$) than others who met the requirements of parole without significant problems. This confirmation of poorer parole adjustment, like that found by Heilbrun and Heilbrun (1985), would be consistent with the dangerousness model. It appears that the impact of prison has less positive effect upon the dangerous sex-criminal who continues to find it difficult to adhere to rules of conduct when he leaves prison. Again, validation proved possible whatever type of sex-offender was being considered -- the generally more dangerous rapist or the generally less dangerous offenders against children.

The most informative way to consider whether the two criteria of dangerousness, criminal recidivism and parole outcome, are independently related to dangerousness is to consider both variables in the same analysis. The main question to be answered would be whether the criminal who demonstrates both prior recidivism and subsequent failure on parole is more dangerous in terms of the model than another who shows a continuing risk for harm in only one of these ways (or in neither way). If so, some independence of relationship between these criteria of risk and dangerousness would be demonstrated.

Table 6 allows us to examine the dangerousness of sex-offenders who were both recidivists before they went to prison and unsuccessful on parole after they left, using the cut-off for parole outcome from the previous analysis. These men are compared with other sex-offenders showing less evidence of continuing risk. The intermediate group showed only one type of continuing criminal risk, and the remaining men were culpable of neither. The results were impressively strong not only in terms of statistical significance ($p<.001$) of the differences among the average dangerousness scores but also in terms of very large absolute differences in these scores. The progressive increase in dangerousness scores as the markers of risk continuity increased from

Table 6: Dangerousness of Sex-Offenders Displaying Various Combinations of Prior Recidivism and Unsuccessful Parole Adjustment

Both a Recidivist and Unsuccessful on Parole		Either a Recidivist or Unsuccessful on Parole		Neither a Recidivist nor Unsuccessful on Parole	
N	M	N	M	N	M
19	3012.53	119	2713.45	131	2299.72

0 to 1 to 2 serves to further validate the dangerousness model and to do so in a convincing fashion. One encouraging fact emerged from this analysis for a beleaguered public. The very high dangerousness and the presence of both types of continuing risk were observed in only about 7% of the sex-offender group.

Prison Conduct as a Criterion of Dangerousness

Incarceration may serve several purposes; rehabilitation, punishment, and isolation as a protection for society are most prominently mentioned. Certainly the noblest among these is the rehabilitation motive that would have us modify the criminal's behavior so that he or she would become a better prospect for living within society's laws and moral code of conduct. The evidence on parole outcome and recidivism that has been presented in this chapter certainly suggests that prisoners deemed more dangerous by the model are not influenced to the same degree as their less dangerous peers by incarceration and institutional efforts to modify their behavior in a prosocial direction. Either that or more dangerous criminals simply have further to go in changing their behavior and are not influenced enough to achieve institutional goals. All I can discern from our own evidence is that very dangerous men go into prison as sex-offending recidivists, indicating that prior incarceration has not deterred their criminality, and come out only to flounder on parole. At this point, I will take a more direct look at whether the more dangerous criminal is less amenable to prosocial change while he is behind prison walls.

The particular criterion of prosocial response to prison that we have studied is the prisoner's record of accommodation to institutional rules of conduct (Heilbrun & Heilbrun, 1985). We were especially interested in the restraint shown by the prisoner from engaging in violent behaviors or behaviors that can be conducive to violence in prison. Reasoning underlying this choice is simple. Prisoners are incarcerated because they have failed to respect the laws of society in general and the rights of individual victims in particular. The goal of the criminal justice system, to the extent that rehabilitation is emphasized, is to return these prisoners to society prepared to follow the dictates of law and to avoid harming others. What better indication of prosocial change in the prisoner is there than the extent to which he accommodates to institutional rules in general and exerts restraint over violence in particular?

I need no reminder that prisoners are cognizant of the link between misconduct in prison and the possibility of serving a longer period of incarceration -- the "bad actor" may be deemed less well prepared for parole. Good conduct, then, might seem to serve a superficial and purely selfish motive of leaving prison earlier and not to represent any real change in the prisoner's value system with respect to rule conformity. I believe this argument misses the point. Criminals, at least the dangerous criminals who have been the subject of my research, break the law in large measure because they lack the values of society at large. What was left to them as a deterrent in the absence of conscience, fear of punishment, failed to constrain their criminality. It would be hard to imagine anyone seriously contending that incarceration serves to institute a constructive value system for criminals so that they emerge from prison on a moral high-ground. A more realistic hope would be that criminals leave the aversive prison experience with a healthier respect for the unpleasant consequences of violating laws of society. If they do, anticipation of punishment can serve as a deterrent to crime. A poor conduct record in prison that results in frequent and/or severe disciplinary action indicates a failure to generate concern about undesirable consequences of rule infraction. The "bad actor" in prison appears to be all the more incorrigible, because his conduct may threaten his timetable for release.

The Heilbrun and Heilbrun study of dangerousness in prison considered a sample of 198 male prisoners housed in the Georgia system. A scale of prison misconduct was devised with rating points ranging from 1 to 7. Scale values increased as more serious violations of the institutional code were encountered and, at its extreme, the scale involved progressively severe threats or demonstrations of violence. The seven scale points included the following:

1 =   opposition to rules involving no confrontation with prison staff (e.g., out of assigned area, possession of contraband);

2 =   opposition to rules involving confrontation with prison staff (e.g., failure to follow instructions, insubordination without threat);

3 =   escape;

4 =   verbal aggression (e.g., insubordination with threat, inciting to riot);

5 =   possession of a weapon;

6 =   physical violence (fighting with another prisoner, physical encounter with staff);

7 =   physical violence resulting in death of victim.

The procedure for arriving at a misconduct score was to examine all disciplinary reports filed during the prisoner's current incarceration for which he was found guilty by trial. Each violation was rated for level of misconduct along the 7-point scale. A total misconduct score was defined by the cumulative ratings over all disciplinary reports for each man. These scores ranged in value from 0 for prisoners never found responsible for misconduct to a high of 101. Not surprisingly, there was a relationship between length of incarceration and the total misconduct score, since a circular relationship is to be expected. The longer the prisoner is incarcerated, the greater the opportunity to violate the rules; the more the prisoner violates the rules, the longer he is likely to remain in prison. However, preliminary analysis that controlled for time of incarceration revealed the same relationship between dangerousness and misconduct for short-termers and long-termers.

The sample of prisoners was broken down by levels of dangerousness as evidenced by index scores. A tripartite division into high, intermediate, and low dangerousness was used. In addition, the sample was further subdivided by whether the prisoners had a history of criminal violence ($\underline{N}$=149) or were nonviolent criminals ($\underline{N}$=49). This allowed us to consider whether dangerousness is associated with differences in prison misconduct across the entire spectrum of dangerous criminality.

Table 7 includes the average misconduct scores in prison for violent and nonviolent prisoners at three levels of index-defined dangerousness. There was an effect of dangerousness ($\underline{p}$<.05) whether the prisoner was a violent or nonviolent criminal. More dangerous men had shown more flagrant misconduct in prison, and their violations often involved actual or threatened violence. However, the tabled data are clearly curvilinear; only the prisoners at the highest level of model-defined dangerousness demonstrated gross misconduct. The results, nonetheless, fall in line with those reported previously for criminal recidivism and parole outcome as criteria of continuing risk of harm to the victims of crime. The dangerous criminal, as defined by the model, is more likely to remain a threat to society despite the impact of prison and the rehabilitation efforts of the criminal justice system. This is made clear whether repeated crimes, inability to accommodate to parole, or prison adjustment is examined for evidence of constructive

Table 7: Prison Misconduct for Violent and Nonviolent Criminals at Three Levels of Dangerousness

Level of Dangerousness	Violent Criminals		Nonviolent Criminals	
	$\underline{N}$	$\underline{M}$	$\underline{N}$	$\underline{M}$
High (2727 or>)	45	10.38	22	10.36
Intermediate (2116-2726)	51	5.76	14	2.43
Low (2115 or<)	53	4.79	13	3.46

change.

Table 7 data bearing upon the prison misconduct of nonviolent criminals is of special interest as far as the overall validation of the dangerousness model is concerned. While it has been possible to demonstrate the expected difference in dangerousness between violent and nonviolent criminals, the begrudging nature of this discrimination has received comment on previous pages. I have proposed that the nonviolent criminal ranks include some whose dangerousness puts them at-risk for future violence but for whom circumstances have not as yet been conducive to escalation in the harm they can do. These nonviolent criminals whose dangerousness portends future violence may cloud the discrimination as much as offenders whose violence is better explained by factors other than dangerousness. I already have provided a brief glimpse at the evidence from a prospective study, to be reported in full in a subsequent chapter, that supported this thesis. The evidence showed that if you track nonviolent criminals for a sufficient period after release from prison, the more dangerous among them will resort to violent crime. We now have a second opportunity to observe the nonviolent but presumably highly dangerous criminal demonstrate his potential for more harmful criminality in the future. His prison misconduct, likely involving threat or actuality of violence, strikes an ominous note for his future adherence to social law.

CHAPTER 6

Validating the Theoretical Assumptions of the Dangerousness Model

To this point of exposition in the book the proposed theoretical model of criminal dangerousness has been tested exclusively in terms of predicted relationships with crime -- the character of crimes committed or with the continuing risk of criminality. There has been no effort to address the theoretical assumptions of the model that are used to explain why offenders who are antisocial and impaired in their cognitive and interpersonal functioning commit crimes that prove more harmful to their victims. Actually, these assumptions are simple enough at this point of model development and can be briefly stated.

Antisociality reflects a lack of concern for the laws governing society or for the moral code held by the social mainstream. Disrespect for society's law and ethics of behavior reduces restraint and makes criminal conduct more likely. When antisociality is coupled with flawed cognition that limits the criminal's higher mental processes (reasoning, planning, social insight, self-restraint, logical inference, etc.), the chances increase that the mechanics of the crime will be poorly orchestrated by the criminal. Poor planning could result in greater peril for the victim than was anticipated by the criminal. Cognitive and social limitations also could contribute to greater danger for the victim by the criminal's inclination to bungle the crime. This would be most evident in the criminal transaction with the victim that is likely to deteriorate as the offender proves incapable of dealing with situational demands and other interpersonal complications that arise. Violence may substitute for other alternatives open to the criminal, especially if emotional arousal or intoxication further compromise his meager psychological potential for higher-order cognition.

The assumption that greater antisociality increases the probability of criminal activity is hardly original with me. In fact, this is true almost by definition as antisociality is gauged in important measure by the person's law-breaking behavior. It is the coupling of antisociality with other psychological limitations that represents a different way of understanding criminal dangerousness, and it is these cognitive and social flaws that require most of the model's current theoretical assumptions. In this chapter I shall report evidence bearing upon the presumed limitations of dangerous criminals, first concerning whether they are less socially competent and then with respect to whether they are lacking in cognitive skills. Following that I will present data concerning whether the risk of violence in criminals, presumably fostered by a lack of social and cognitive skills, is associated with deterioration of a criminal transaction for more dangerousness men.

Social Competence and Dangerousness

One of the primary assumptions of the dangerousness model, as I have reiterated in the preceding section, is that limited interpersonal skills of the criminal may result in more serious harm to the victim because transactions falter. I have examined this premise in two ways. One way has been to determine the relationship between social competence (outgoingness versus withdrawal) and criminal dangerousness. Although exceptions could certainly be found, socially-withdrawn people should be more lacking in interpersonal skills than those drawn to social interaction. The absence of skill helps to explain reticence to interact and, in circular fashion, social reticence limits opportunity to improve deficient skills. I first will address the withdrawal/outgoingness line of evidence as social orientation relates to prison conduct. The follow-up analysis of interpersonal skills as they relate to dangerousness will involve an examination of personality test results as the gauge of transactional effectiveness.

Studies of social orientation and dangerousness. The importance of social competence in criminal dangerousness was considered within the Heilbrun and Heilbrun (1985) study of prison misconduct. I already have reported the primary finding that more dangerous men according to the model were responsible for more misconduct while incarcerated as measured by severity ratings of rule violations adjudicated by a prison court. Greater misconduct was considered to be a sign that the prisoner was failing to respond constructively to rehabilitation efforts and remained a continuing risk. We went beyond examining this theoretically basic relationship by introducing sociability as an additional variable to see if the prediction of misconduct could be improved.   Blackburn (1975, 1979) had reported previously upon the role of social orientation in prison behavior as it interacts with psychopathy of the prisoner.

More specifically, Heilbrun and Heilbrun began with the baseline finding that the 58 male prisoners, who qualified as most dangerous after median-split assignment to the high antisociality-low IQ quadrant, had received disciplinary reports for misconduct in prison that had accumulated to an average of 12.90 rating-scale points.   This was singularly high relative to the remaining prisoner groups.   The Sociability scale (Sy) taken from the California Psychological Inventory (CPI) and the Social Introversion scale (Si) from the Minnesota Multiphasic Personality Inventory (MMPI) were used in tandem to quantify the social outgoingness/withdrawal dimension. The subtractive index, Sy-Si, will go up in value with increased sociability of the subject and decrease as social withdrawal is indicated. (Both scales use standard scores with the same general population mean of 50 and the same standard deviation of 10.)   A median split on this subtractive index for the entire sample separated the 58 dangerous prisoners into those who were socially withdrawn (N=36) and who were socially outgoing (N=22).   The remainder of the prisoner sample, who served as controls, provided 80 that were socially withdrawn and 87 that were more outgoing.

The high antisocial-low IQ men who were more socially withdrawn presented a mean misconduct score of 16.36; the high antisocial-low IQ men who were more outgoing had an average score of only 7.23, reliably less ($\underline{p}<.001$).   This differentiating effect of sociability was not observed among the remaining control prisoners. Those who were more socially withdrawn presented a mean misconduct score of 5.58, whereas the more outgoing had an average misconduct score of 4.63.   The negligible difference failed to be statistically significant. Accordingly, the expected relationship between impaired social competence and prison misconduct in the more dangerous prisoner was confirmed, perhaps in even stronger terms than we had reason to expect.   The most dangerous prisoners defied the conduct code of prison rather blatantly but only if they were socially inept; the effect of a withdrawn social orientation was not only less in other prisoners, it was nonexistent.

This pattern of results lends confidence to the assumption that limitations in transacting interpersonally play a role in criminal dangerousness and the risk of victim harm. However, in this analysis the misconduct by the socially-withdrawn, dangerous criminals was directed toward other prisoners and prison staff for the most part rather than the victims of street crimes. We did not record whether the breaches of discipline that went into misconduct scores represented a deterioration of some social transaction that began on a less serious note. However, my experience with reading prisoner files suggests that this is more often the rule than the exception when disciplinary reports are filed.

An even more striking demonstration of the importance of social orientation in understanding victim risk among the most dangerous prisoners was revealed when Heilbrun and Heilbrun further refined their high-antisocial/low IQ subset of male prisoners by reference to prior criminal history. The 36 socially-withdrawn, low-IQ antisocials, isolated as conduct problems in the previous analysis, were further broken down by those who had been convicted of a violent crime ($\underline{N}$=22) and those who had not ($\underline{N}$=14). Prison misconduct scores soared to an average of 19.81 for the former group in contrast to 7.40 for the latter ($\underline{p}$<.001). In other words, if you verify (1) the dangerousness of prisoners by the model, (2) social withdrawal by test scores, and (3) prior victim abuse by violent history, the level of misconduct in prison for those identified reaches singularly disruptive proportions.

In order to attain an average score of 19.81 given the nature of the rating scale, the high antisocial-low IQ, socially-withdrawn, and criminally-violent group had to have engaged in continuing confrontation in prison, some of it involving violence. In stark contrast to the inept social transaction implied by this very high misconduct score, a breakdown of the remaining prisoners by prior criminal violence and social withdrawal did not reveal anything. Men who were criminally violent and socially withdrawn but not dangerous by model specifications had conduct records ($\underline{M}$=5.68) much like the remainder of the sample ($\underline{M}$=4.09).

Some years later in 1990, Allison Foster and Jill Golden contributed to the research program by collecting a sample of male sex-offenders (rapists and child molesters) from the backlog of parole assessment cases. I have found the MMPI and CPI results that were made available to be useful in many ways as assumptions of the dangerousness model are considered. Right now, these test profiles offer an opportunity to substantiate the 1985 findings that high antisocial-low IQ men in prison can be separated into those who are singular transactional risks if socially withdrawn but who resemble other prisoners in their level of misconduct if socially outgoing.

The procedure followed in analyzing this 1990 sample was to first separate the 119 sex-offenders, about half rapists and half child molesters, into three levels of dangerousness based upon the quantitative index. The Sy-Si score in this analysis was used to establish social orientation, as was the case in the 1985 study, but this time Sy-Si was used as the dependent variable. That being the case, it is important to point out again that the subtractive formula of Sy-Si should provide increments in positive scores as social outgoingness increases and higher negative scores as increasing social withdrawal is encountered. An additional social-transactional scale from the CPI was available for analysis as well. Social Presence (Sp) scores promised to reveal what the effectiveness of transaction would be if an individual were involved in a social interaction, criminal or otherwise. This scale was devised as a measure of "poise, spontaneity, and self-confidence" within social relationships (Gough, 1957).

Table 8 presents the social orientation and social presence comparisons for male prisoners at three levels of dangerousness. Examination of the means for the Sy-Si index shows their order to be consistent with the theoretical model. The most dangerous were especially withdrawn; the least dangerous were quite outgoing; and intermediate dangerousness was associated with in-between status as mildly outgoing. Statistics confirmed the reliability of these differences (P<.001). The Sp means also were in the predicted order with the lowest Social Presence scores found in the most dangerous men. The differences between dangerousness groups were significant (p<.05). These psychometric findings are consistent with the assumption of the model that the dangerousness of the more highly antisocial and less cognitively competent criminal involves his limited ability to interact with people. This is the same conclusion drawn from the Heilbrun and Heilbrun (1985) prison misconduct evidence.

Control analyses for the social orientation findings. Since the 1990 data bearing upon social-transactional skills in prisoners at

Table 8: Dangerousness and Traits Related to Effective Social Interaction in Sex-offending Criminals

	Dangerousness		
Social Trait	High (N=40)	Intermediate (N=41)	Low (N=38)
	M	M	M
Outgoingness/Withdrawal[a]	-6.32	4.68	9.00
Social Presence	45.30	48.27	52.34

[a] *Given by subtraction of Si scores from Sy scores; increases in the plus direction indicate greater outgoingness, and increases in the minus direction point to greater withdrawal.*

varying levels of dangerousness came from self-report questionnaires administered as part of parole assessment, the question of whether efforts at dissimulation played a role in the results might be raised. This seems as good a place as any to address this kind of concern. Each of the personality tests includes a scale geared to measure "fake good" responses to the items. The Lie (L) scale of the MMPI and Good Impression (Gi) scale of the CPI were devised specifically for this purpose. The sum of these two scales (each being standardized with the same mean and standard deviation) should represent a good gauge of positive dissimulation, and the correlation between this dissimulation score and the scales involved in the social transaction analyses allow for a closer look at whether testing conditions influenced test results. As it turned out, neither of the correlations was statistically significant nor of much magnitude; (L+Gi) versus Social Presence, r=.06;(L+Gi) versus (Sy-Si), r=.17. The test results suggesting that more dangerous criminals are more socially inept cannot be readily explained in terms of test response set, since these social variables share but 0-3% common variance with the index of dissimulation.

A second question that might be raised about the results of the 1990 social-transaction analysis would bear upon the types of criminals that we elected to examine. The choice of sex-offenders was a considered one. The crimes of rape and child molestation represent examples of violent crime in which the criminal and victim are likely to be involved in a close and complicated interaction, especially rape. Impaired skills on the part of the criminal could introduce special risk of escalating violence as he plays out his coercive role. However, the restriction of the sample to sex-offenders might raise the question of whether they are representative of criminals who have engaged in transactional violence without an obvious link to sex. A control group of 56 men convicted of aggravated assault or assault-with-intent-to-murder offenses was collected from the parole-assessment file in order to establish whether social effectiveness was related to dangerousness when other than sex-offenders were considered. Victims of criminal assault could be either a woman or another man.

A parallel analysis to that reported for sex-offenders was conducted. Table 9 presents the average Sy-Si and Sp scores obtained from men found guilty of serious assault charges after being broken down into tripartite levels of dangerousness. The same order of mean values was obtained in the control analysis of men convicted of assault

Table 9: Dangerousness and traits Related to Effective Social Interaction (Assault Cases)

	Dangerousness		
Social Trait	High (N=18)	Intermediate (N=18)	Low (N=20)
	M	M	M
Outgoingness/Withdrawal[a]	-7.10	-3.28	6.70
Social Presence	46.15	47.06	51.67

[a] See footnote to Table 8.

as was evident with sex-offenders, and the variation was significant for both social outgoingness/withdrawal ($p<.01$) and social-presence ($p<.05$). The most dangerous violent criminals were socially withdrawn and had the poorest social presence; the least dangerous were socially outgoing and had the best social presence. Intermediate dangerousness was associated with in-between scores on both social variables. Transactional deficits of the more dangerous violent criminal are not restricted to sex-offenders. They are evident as well in men who physically assault their victims without evident sexual intent.

The core theoretical assumptions of the dangerousness model state that impaired moral/legal restraint in the antisocial individual increases the probability that a criminal act will occur and that limited skill in social transaction increases the risk of violence for the victim of the crime. The data reported in this section are certainly consistent with the thesis that dangerous men are more socially withdrawn and interpersonally inept. Furthermore, interpersonal inadequacies were identified in dangerous men who were convicted of crimes in which social transactions most likely deteriorated into physical aggression (assault). The role of social limitations may be the most alarming in contact sex offenses in which criminal transactions are especially vulnerable to escalating risk. The interactive nature of the crime and the possibility of victim resistance to the coercive act may rapidly exceed the transactional competence of the criminal, specially in the case of rape and the victimization of an adult woman. The broader ramifications of the role of social inadequacies in the risk of violence for the dangerous criminal came when social incompetence was tied to serious prison misconduct as well as street crime.

Cognition and Dangerousness

The social-transaction variables that were considered in the previous section represent obvious descriptors of interpersonal competence. Whether criminals tend to turn away from people or lack poise and self-confidence in direct dealings with others tell us something of how ineffective they might be when dealing with the victim in a criminal context.

In this section emphasis will be shifted to cognition and dangerousness and to that part of the theory which depends upon the assumption of flawed mental operations to explain increased risk of violence. The evidence to be examined will be more specific in one sense compared to the broad social parameters that were used to estimate transactional effectiveness of the very dangerous criminal. Cognitive analysis considered discrete variables rather than broad-gauge parameters of social behavior.

The flawed cognition of the dangerous offender has been linked to increased risk of violence at two stages of criminal activity. Anticipation of criminal activity by the dangerous offender is less likely to involve the quality of planning and judgment that could avert confrontation with the victim if that were intended. In theory that could result from the diminished planning/judgment capabilities of the dangerous criminal or from the impulsive nature of the crime that precludes planning and judgment, probably both. Actual commission of the crime for the dangerous criminal would place the victim at greater risk, because cognitive limitations of the offender make it more likely that he will resort to more serious extremes than the situation requires, even for criminal ends. Robberies turn to physical assault, contact sex-offenses escalate into more life-threatening physical aggression, and burglaries/auto thefts become violent when discovery threatens capture. For the most part, the cognitive deficits to be considered could contribute to risk at either stage of the crime. As an example, inadequate impulse control could result in a poorly-orchestrated crime or in a failure to restrain violent actions during the conduct of a crime.

Impulse control, empathy, and dangerousness. Heilbrun's (1982) study of cognitive models for criminal violence offers an initial opportunity to examine two cognitive variables that are clearly relevant to the behavior of the criminal in contemplating a crime and/or toward a victim in the conduct of his crime. One of these variables, impulse control, was measured in three different ways using a sample of 46 male prisoners. The first of these involved summing two error scores taken from performance on laboratory tasks; this score was labeled "cognitive control." Both tasks involved the same principle; expose the subject to a condition in which he has a habitual mode of response to a particular set of cues, and then instruct him to respond in an unusual way to the same cues. Cognitive control represents how well he curbs his inclination to act out of habit by self-instruction. The two other impulse-control measures were taken from personality tests -- the Hypomania (Ma) scale of the MMPI and the Self-control (Sc) scale of the CPI.

Empathy represented the second cognitive variable under investigation and was measured by the Empathy scale (Hogan, 1969), a collection of items related to empathic behavior taken from the MMPI and CPI. High scorers are described by Hogan as "socially acute and sensitive to nuances in interpersonal behavior," whereas low scorers are considered as "hostile, cold and insensitive to the feelings of others." Empathy, then, involves the ability to identify the feelings of others and to use them in understanding interpersonal behavior.

Now what about the relevance of these cognitive variables to the conduct of a crime? Poor impulse control, as I have already said by way of illustration, would increase the risk for unbridled expression of violence in the criminal transaction just as it placed the victim at greater risk because of inadequate planning. Empathic deficit would make the criminal less sensitive to victim distress and tend to reduce whatever sympathy he might have for the victim. It also would make it more likely that he would mislabel the victim's feelings and intent to resist. Violence could represent an inappropriate and unnecessary counteractive measure.

Subject data in the 1982 Heilbrun study were analyzed in keeping with the procedures of the early dangerousness studies. Prisoners were assigned to one of four antisociality-IQ groups based upon median split of the sample distributions. My special interest, of course, was in the anticipated cognitive limitations of the high antisociality-low IQ subgroup of prisoners who represented a singularly high level of dangerousness according to theory. Table 10 presents the impulse-control findings for this study and includes the average scores of the four antisociality-IQ groupings on the three measures. Examination of the mean scores reveals the greater impulsivity of the high antisocial-low IQ criminal on each of the three measures relative to the other subgroups. Criminals who were by definition the most dangerous were consistently the most impulsive. The high error score on the cognitive-control tasks (M=116.00) was reliably greater than the other subgroups combined (M=96.86,p<.05). The Hypomania scale results revealed the high scores of the index group (M=64.45) in significant excess of those for the combined group (M=57.09,p<.05). The mean Self-control score for the high antisocial-low IQ subgroup (M=48.82) fell reliably below that of the remaining criminals combined (M=56.19,p<.05).

The empathy results, based upon 119 prisoners and reported in Table 11, are not as clearly supportive of the dangerousness model as

Table 10: Impulse Control for Criminals Separated by Level of Antisociality and IQ

Level of Antisociality and Impulse Control Variable	Level of IQ	
	High IQ	Low IQ
	M	M
High Antisociality		
Laboratory tasks[a]	95.30	116.00
Hypomania scale[b]	59.56	64.45
Self-control scale[c]	53.50	48.82
Low Antisociality		
Laboratory tasks	88.92	106.75
Hypomania scale	54.62	57.92
Self-control scale	57.75	57.00

Note: The number of subjects in each group were: High antisociality-high IQ = 10, high antisociality-low IQ = 11, low antisociality-high IQ = 13, low antisociality-low IQ = 12.
 [a] *Higher scores indicate poorer impulse control.*
 [b] *Higher scores indicate poorer impulse control.*
 [c] *Lower scores indicate poorer impulse control.*

Table 11: Empathy Scores for Prisoners Varying in Antisociality and IQ

Level of Antisociality	Level of IQ			
	High		Low	
	$\underline{N}$	$\underline{M}$	$\underline{N}$	$\underline{M}$
High	27	30.19	32	25.72
Low	35	29.06	25	25.64

were the impulse-control findings. There was a significant effect for intelligence based upon the lower empathy scores for both low-IQ prisoner groups ($p < .01$). This finding, in retrospect at least, is not hard to explain in light of the psychological nature of empathy. It has been argued that this skill depends upon a kind of "motor mimicry" in which the observer experiences the same emotional response as the observed person; by experiencing the same emotion, the observer can identify the other person's feelings. Whether mimicry is involved or not, it remains true that accurate identification of another person's emotions requires recognition and integration of a number of cues gained from facial expression, bodily posture, verbal communication, and situational circumstances. All of these would factor into the summary judgment. Hogan's scale takes empathy beyond this point to where it allows for appreciation of fine distinctions in interpersonal behavior. That criminals who are not very bright lack this skill across the board comes as no surprise.

If both the impulse-control and empathy results are considered together, it is still possible to make a case for support of the dangerousness model despite the rather oblique nature of the empathy evidence. The most dangerous subset of criminals was distinguished from other offenders by their more pervasive cognitive impairment. High-antisocial/low IQ men were the only ones to combine impulsivity with low empathy, thereby promising the highest degree of criminal risk.

Higher mental processes, impulse control and dangerousness. The more recent Foster-Golden sample of sex-offenders, collected in 1990, proved useful in examining the specific cognitive properties of dangerous criminals as these would be represented on personality tests. The CPI includes two scales that are of special interest in examining the cognitive assets and liabilities that may influence criminal conduct. Gough's (1957) instrument offers us the Intellectual Efficiency (Ie) scale for one. This scale goes beyond measured IQ to portray the extent to which the individual makes functional use of intelligence possessed. The correlation between Ie and IQ was only .09 within this sample of criminals, so Ie as a personality scale does not simply reiterate the results of a standard metric of intelligence. Extreme scorers on this scale are described by Gough as clear-thinking, planful, resourceful, and as placing high value on cognitive and intellectual matters at the high end. These are the last qualities I would expect to find in the confused, shallow, and lacking in self-direction and self-discipline; these flawed qualities are more in line with dangerousness according to theory. My expectation, then, was that the most dangerous criminals, already identified as limited in intelligence as measured by IQ, would show themselves to be even more restricted in their higher mental functions by less efficient use of what intelligence is available to them.

The second CPI scale of interest was Psychological-Mindedness (Py), the degree to which the individual is interested in and sensitive to the needs, motives, and experiences of others. This variable shows some conceptual overlap with empathy as Hogan defined the term, but there is a difference in emphasis. Empathy has traditionally been understood as the ability to share the emotions of others in a vicarious way and through shared experience and the processing of other relevant cues to better comprehend what another person is feeling. Gough's Py variable places greater emphasis upon the astute and resourceful appraisal of individual behavior in a social context -- another person's or your own. Used in this way, psychological-mindedness describes a broader range of observation and judgment in interpersonal transaction and is somewhat akin to social intelligence. Prediction here should be obvious; more dangerous criminals should present lower Py scores.

Table 12 includes the Ie and Py scale means for three levels of dangerousness in sex-offenders. The progression of mean values is in the predicted order for both sets of means, and the variation of means was significant for both Ie ($p<.001$) and Py ($p<.05$). The pattern of findings points toward cognitive limitations of the more dangerous criminal. His IQ, already measured as low by a standard intelligence test, actually seems to overestimate the intellectual capabilities that he can bring to bear in the conduct of crime sponsored by high antisociality. This limited utilization of all-too-meager intelligence resources would detract from the dangerous criminal's ability to plan a violence-free crime or to conduct one. Further, the dangerous criminal's restricted grasp of the behavioral dynamics within the criminal transaction, suggested by lower psychological-mindedness, would add further to the danger of a deteriorating confrontation with the victim. A halting understanding of what the victim's behavior really means is made even more likely when you remember that the lower psychological-mindedness of the dangerous offender is probably going to be accompanied by diminished empathic skill.

This study of sex-offender personality-test profiles collected in

Table 12: Dangerousness and Cognitive Traits Contributing to Effective Planning and Conduct of Crime (Sex-Offenders)

Cognitive Trait	Dangerousness		
	High (N=40) M	Intermediate (N=41) M	Low (N=38) M
Intellectual Efficiency	38.78	45.78	52.84
Psychological-Mindedness	48.52	49.80	54.10

1990 also allowed me to attempt a replication of the earlier impulse-control findings. The Self-control (Sc) scale of the CPI and the Hypomania (Ma) scale from the MMPI both demonstrated greater impulsivity for the most dangerous criminals as part of the 1982 study, in line with laboratory tasks and theory. For simplicity sake, I combined these scale scores into a single impulse-control score, Sc minus Ma. The higher the score, the better the control of impulses. Theory and earlier results led me to expect higher dangerousness to be associated with poorer impulse control. This was confirmed when the 40 men with the highest dangerousness scores showed up as most poorly controlled ($\underline{M}$=-10.46), the intermediate dangerousness group of 41 criminals as somewhat better in this regard ($\underline{M}$=-4.38), and the 38 low dangerousness sex-offenders revealing the best self-control ($\underline{M}$=2.10), ($\underline{p}$<.001).

Characteristics of the Crime, Risk of Deterioration into Violence, and Dangerousness

Information available from prisoner files includes details regarding circumstances of the crime and behavior of the criminal and victim during the conduct of the crime. Some of this information appears to be relevant to the theoretical assumption that dangerousness invokes added risk of violence because criminal transaction with the victim takes a turn for the worse. Characteristics of the crime that were abstracted from the file include intoxication of the criminal, resistance of the victim and use of force by the criminal, and the evolution of violence in the context of some less severe crime. Anyone familiar with criminal files will probably agree that sections on circumstance are not constituted with research in mind. Ratings by trained judges were required to quantify specific characteristics and reliability checks were deemed necessary. These agreement coefficients turned out to be consistently between .60 and .90, usually nearer the higher figure, so I have some degree of confidence in these difficult ratings.

Intoxication and dangerousness. The level of intoxication of child molesters at the time their sexual offenses were committed received attention in an earlier attempt to explain the variability of dangerousness within this sex-offender group. Dangerous child molesters, as defined by the model, were found to be more intoxicated when they accosted their victims. This would add further risk for the child because of the disinhibitory effects of intoxication upon dangerous men who tend to lack restraint in the first place. At this point, I want to extend this analysis to all of the sex-offenders in the Hollmann (1990) and Wasieleski (1990) samples and to apply the findings in a more general way to the dangerousness model.

Analysis proceeded by separating each of the four male sex-offender groups (rapists, heterosexual child molesters, homosexual child molesters, and perpetrators of incest) into those who were rated as being intoxicated to any degree during their crime (mildly to greatly) and those who were judged to be sober. The dangerousness scores of intoxicated and nonintoxicated men within the sex-offender groups are found in Table 13.

There are two things to notice as far as Table 13 data are concerned. The first has to do with the numbers of sex-offenders within each group that are under some degree of alcohol or drug influence at the time of their offenses. The most dangerous sex-offender group (rapists), as shown by index score and crime severity table, demonstrated an intoxication rate of 67%. At the other extreme, the least dangerous group (homosexual child molesters) committed their sexual offenses while inebriated in only 23% of the cases. The sex-offender groups that showed intermediate levels of dangerousness according to the model and their crimes also posted intermediate percentages of men who were intoxicated when their sexual crimes were committed. Some 47% of the child molesters targeting female children and 40% of the men who committed incest with girls in their family were intoxicated to some degree when their crimes occurred. Nonparametric analysis showed these proportional differences to be significant (p<.001). The more dangerous the type of sex-offender, the more likely he will act while inebriated.

Table 13 also demonstrates the contingency between dangerousness in sex-offenders and intoxication at the time of the crime in another way and even more emphatically. All four sex-offender groups demonstrated the same effect no matter how serious their sexual crimes. Sex-offenders who were intoxicated during the offense, whether it is rape, child molestation, or incest, were found to have higher dangerousness scores than their sober counterparts. Statistical analysis confirmed the apparent link between intoxication and dangerousness across all types of sex-offenders (p<.01).

The manner in which the intoxication findings support the assumptions of the dangerousness model has received mention but bears

Table 13: Dangerousness and Intoxication of Sex-Offenders During the Crime

			Type of Sex-Offense					
Intoxication Level	Rape		Heterosexual Child Molestation		Homosexual Child Molestation		Incest	
	N	M	N	M	N	M	N	M
Intoxicated[a]	38	2880.60	62	2673.64	6	2478.67	18	2675.06
Not intoxicated	19	2511.42	69	2339.38	20	1856.60	27	2179.45

a   *Including ratings from "mildly" through "greatly"*

repetition. Risk to the victim increases as dangerousness increases, because the cognitive underpinnings of effective action are found lacking. Alcohol and drug effects could only serve to further compromise these skills given the expected influence of inebriation upon higher cortical functions. Intoxication in otherwise dangerous criminals should result in even less restraint over antisocial tendencies and even more haphazard planning of the crimes that follow. With social competence already flawed, intoxication also would tend to produce a further decrement in the dangerous man's ability to deal effectively with the criminal-victim interaction. The combination of dangerousness and intoxication would seriously interfere with emotional control, consideration of alternative actions, comprehending victim reactions, or using good judgment to mention only some transactional skills.

The examination of intoxication effects in sex-offenders disclosed two things that are important as far as victim risk is concerned. Contact sex-offenders of all types who act while inebriated are more dangerous to begin with than their sober counterparts. Accordingly, intoxication as a common feature of sexual aggression is likely to contribute to substantial cognitive impairment, because it will be associated with dangerousness. To make matters worse, the tendency for dangerous sex-offenders to act while intoxicated becomes stronger as more severe types of sex-offenses are considered. The worst-case scenario is provided by rapists. Men who rape while intoxicated are not only the most dangerous sex-offenders as evidenced by index score and their type of sexual crime, but the combination of dangerousness and inebriation is found in a far higher percentage of cases. It would follow that our concern about cognitive impairment in the dangerous criminal and victim harm should be directed primarily toward rapists.

Brutality in criminal violence and dangerousness--the role of victim resistance in rape. Analysis of criminal behavior for men committing the same nominal violent crimes (rape or murder) revealed that the more dangerous among them exposed victims to excesses of brutality. In reporting these within-crime findings, I was aware that brutal treatment of the victim need not be considered solely in terms of the offender's attributes. Violent behavior may evolve out of transactional circumstances in which the criminal's goal is thwarted by resistance of the victim. Resistance to being victimized can successfully thwart a crime, but it also may prompt any number of effects that increase risk for the victim. It may evoke greater force from the criminal to achieve his ends; arouse emotional responses of frustration, anger, or fear in the criminal provoking violent action; or add a complication to the transactional circumstances that lends confusion to the judgment and decision-making of the criminal. In short, resistance on the part of a victim, however warranted, may be in part responsible for the cruel exercise of force or aggression in the conduct of crime. As the criminal escalates force or aggression, resistance from the victim may increase in turn as a means of self-protection. Brutality and resistance, then, are likely to be reciprocal. The extent to which brutal violence can be explained in terms of victim resistance as opposed to being a property of criminal dangerousness remains an open question.

Rape represents a crime often involving victim resistance that might trigger extra force or aggression on the part of the criminal. The crime represents a severe breach of the woman's right to privacy and respect that is violated by forced intimate sexual contact. Efforts to stop this intrusion would be expected unless the woman were fearful of even more serious harm than sexual violation. Not only would women be expected to resist being raped in substantial numbers, but you may recall that rapists, as the most dangerous sex-offenders, would be especially ill-prepared to deal with resistance except by brute force according to our data. Cognitive impairment further compromised by intoxication is commonly found in dangerous rapists, and this combination leaves him few alternatives to hurtful force. Analyzing brutality of the criminal, victim resistance, and dangerousness as they coalesce in the act of rape seemed especially appropriate.

The expected reciprocal nature of resistance and force in the act of rape raises a thorny methodological issue. How can these behaviors of the victim and the criminal be teased apart in order to extricate them from their reciprocal relationship for purpose of study? I found it possible to do this even with static file information concerning the criminal circumstances of rape. At least it will be possible to establish whether more brutal sexual aggression is to some extent inherent in the dangerous rapist, not to be explained fully as a result of victim resistance. How this is done will be made clear as I proceed in describing an unpublished study of rapist violence.

A new sample of 142 male rapists was collected using prisoner files as the source of information regarding the circumstances of the crime and to establish components of the dangerousness index.

Brutality scores were based upon two separate ratings made by trained assistants. One involved physical harm inflicted upon the victim with a scale extending from 0 (very little harm) to 4 (very severe harm). The second rating considered psychological intimidation and was generated on a similar 5-point scale ranging from 0 (very little intimidation) to 4 (very severe intimidation). These ratings were summed in each case to provide an overall picture of victim mistreatment during the rape by physical aggression and psychological threat. Resistance of the victim was judged along another 5-point scale, 0 (very little resistance) to 4 (very serious resistance).

One way to disentangle the brutality of dangerous rapists from the efforts to resist by the victim is to examine the relationship between brutality and resistance at varying levels of dangerousness. In principle, the greater the potential for harming the victim that the dangerous rapist brings to the crime because of his personality flaws, the less he requires the provocation of resistance to conduct the rape in a brutal way. This principle would direct our attention more to the nature of sexual aggression when the woman does not offer much resistance than to how the rapist responds to strenuous resistance. Two types of analysis were performed to allow for this.

If the amount of brutality introduced into the sexual assault by the more dangerous rapist showed less regard for victim resistance, the correlation between brutality and victim opposition should continue to fall as higher levels of dangerousness are examined. The overall correlation between ratings of rapist brutality and victim resistance for the entire sample was .55 ($p<.001$), confirming the general reciprocity of the two behaviors. When the rapists were broken down into three levels of dangerousness by a tripartite division of the sample distribution, the following correlations were obtained: low dangerousness (N=48),r=.70; intermediate dangerousness (N=47),r=.54; high dangerousness (N=47),r=.41. The progression of correlations from high to low dangerousness was linear, and the difference between these correlations proved significant ($p<.05$) when the correlational extremes were compared. Brutality of the rape proved to be less contingent on victim resistance as more dangerous rapists were considered. These correlation results suggest that the exercise of brutal violence is more a part of victim risk brought to the sex-offense by the dangerous rapist and less a response of the criminal to victim resistance. However, analysis by central tendencies is necessary in order to reach this conclusion with confidence.

The relationships between dangerousness, rapist brutality, and victim resistance were examined next by comparing average levels of brutality. I kept the same three levels of dangerousness for the rapists but broke each level down by how much resistance the victim had offered to being raped. A split nearest the sample median resulted in high resistance being defined by ratings at scale points 3 to 5 with low resistance defined by points 0 to 2. Table 14 presents the average brutality scores for the three levels of dangerousness and the two levels of resistance.

Statistical analysis of the Table 14 data revealed effects of dangerousness ($p<.05$) and resistance ($p<.001$); more dangerous rapists were more brutal in their conduct of the rape, and women who offered more resistance were dealt with in a more brutal way. Examined by degree of victim resistance, however, we can see that men at all levels of dangerousness presented high brutality scores (6.32-6.75) when the women showed stronger resistance. However, in the face of less resistance, brutality varied more widely across dangerousness groups (2.81-4.70) with the most dangerous men displaying the highest degree of brutality ($p>.05$). These findings suggest that the predictability of rape brutality from victim resistance for more dangerous rapists falls below that found for other rapists, because these dangerous men show disproportionate brutality when the woman offers only token resistance or even no discernible resistance at all. Increments of harm to the victims of rape despite only modest resistance or less must be explained by the character of the dangerous rapist.

The question of why the most dangerous rapists would brutalize their victims more despite little resistance on the part of the women cannot be answered in a definitive way by the data we collected even if we narrow the possibilities to attributes of the criminal. One possibility would fall more in line with efforts to explain the act of rape by emphasizing nonsexual motivation rather than orgastic sexual need. Explanations might portray the excesses of brutality as predicated upon the need to dominate women, hostility toward women, or the sexual excitement generated by inflicting pain (sadism). This line of explanation bears no special relevance to the dangerousness model as far as I have gone with it, but that does not mean that dangerousness in rapists might not be somehow linked to psychological problems that men have in their relationships with women.

Another approach to understanding the present results comes

Table 14: Dangerousness, Resistance of the Victim, and Brutality of Rape

| Victim Resistance | Dangerousness | | | | | |
| | High | | Intermediate | | Low | |
	N	M	N	M	N	M
High	20	6.75	18	6.44	22	6.32
Low	27	4.70	29	3.75	26	2.81

closer to what has been proposed in terms of deficiencies in cognitive and social skills within the dangerousness model. The added physical harm and intimidation of the dangerous rapist in the face of token victim resistance could stem from his impaired ability to make social discriminations and to transact interpersonally with others. His lack of empathy, social judgment, psychological-mindedness, and self-control, to mention only variables I have studied, could seriously limit the dangerous rapist's ability to anticipate what the female victim intends to do or even to properly appreciate what she is actually doing. Impaired ability to discern when force is required and limited control over its unnecessary use would lend themselves to brutality in cases where little resistance is met. By this analysis, it is not so much that the dangerous rapist lets the sexual crime deteriorate into even more serious violence when the woman resists. All rapists tend to respond with excessive brutality in the face of obvious and strenuous victim resistance. The dangerous rapist is not astute enough in his social perceptions to recognize token resistance for what it is and that his criminal goals can be achieved without brutality.

Dangerousness and violence evolving within the context of another crime. Another way to look at the dangerousness model in terms of its specific assumptions is to consider whether criminal dangerousness predicts violence that erupts in the conduct of another crime. I shall now examine murder that occurs in the course of committing another offense such as rape, kidnapping, robbery, or burglary. This analysis bears upon the assumption of the theoretical model that violence on the part of the dangerous criminal often depends upon his inability to plan or conduct an effective criminal transaction because of his cognitive limitations. Poor planning or bungled conduct of one crime may result in violence or the escalation of violence, in this case murder.

The data required for this analysis were taken from the Heilbrun (1990b) study of death-sentence and life-sentence murderers already reported in the chapter on within-crime comparisons. One type of rating obtained from the files during that investigation considered whether the murder in any given case occurred in the course of committing another crime. A 4-point probability scale was employed with anchoring points at "definitely not," "possibly not," "possibly," and "definitely." These ratings were used to separate murderers into those who were possibly not or definitely not involved in another crime when they killed their victims and those who possibly or definitely were engaged in another crime when the murder occurred. The previous separation of the murderers by life sentence or death penalty was maintained.

Table 15 includes dangerousness scores for the four groups formed by criminal context for the murder and by sentence. The results were clear. Whatever the sentence, men who likely killed their victims while committing some lesser crime were more dangerous than murderers whose killings probably occurred independently of another crime ($p<.01$). These findings are consistent with those revealed by the rape analysis. The dangerous man is not only a risk because he engages in violent criminal activities to begin with but an even greater risk to the victim because he tends to become violent or to step up his violence within the criminal transaction. In the analysis of murderers, the more dangerous men allowed their violence to reach deadly proportions.

Table 15: Dangerousness and Murder Occurring Within Another Crime by Death-sentence and Life-sentence Murderers

Sentence	Murder Definitely or Probably Within Context of Another Crime		Murder Definitely or Probably Not Within Context of Another Crime	
	N	M	N	M
Death	47	2733.13	19	2342.47
Life in Prison	56	2553.43	72	2240.67

CHAPTER 7

The Long-term Prediction of Criminally Dangerous Behavior - A Critical Study

The issue of what would make one study a more critical test of the dangerousness model than another may hinge upon a number of considerations that need not concern us at this point. I will offer my own opinion without trying to argue that another version of crucial validation could not have been instituted. The signature study in our program, reported in this chapter, had to satisfy three requirements.

For one, the study had to be entirely prospective; predictions regarding dangerous behavior from one point in time had to be projected to some future point of reference. True prediction, a valued commodity within measurement research, is represented among the various relationships reported in this book. However, the use of true prediction has been limited by the methodology of the research program. The substantial number of studies required for systematic research of criminal behavior tended to rule out a prospective methodology, particularly if longer-term prediction were necessary. The time necessary to await the results of one crime investigation, as dangerousness is measured and future predictions are checked out, would introduce too much delay before the results could be analyzed and the next related study could be planned. Besides, a prospective methodology would have precluded prior criminal behavior as a source of validation for the dangerousness model, and this proved to be a valuable source of evidence. The best I could do in the studies reported up to this point was to include a modest prospective slant when prison conduct for men varying in dangerousness was considered, as some of the prison misconduct was recorded after dangerousness scores were assigned, and to make all parole outcome data prospective in nature.

Although the prediction of any criminal behavior was deemed important, I considered it especially critical to determine whether dangerousness scores would relate to future violent crime. Given the lower rate of occurrence for violent offenses relative to property crime, prediction would have to contend with the problems of anticipating rare psychological events. Others who have attempted the prediction of violence (Wenk, Robinson, & Smith, 1972) have concluded that their effort failed in part because of a low baserate in the community. However, future criminal violence would not be as rare in the population of confirmed criminals that served as my research pool as it would be in a normal population, so baserate does not qualify automatically as an excuse for failure. Of course, the importance of predicting criminal violence goes well beyond demonstrating the power of the dangerousness model by anticipating low-frequency events. The special peril of violent crime to a lawful society has been a persistent theme in this book; it stands to reason that identification of criminals at higher risk for future violence should be given priority.

A third requirement for a critical study of the dangerousness model was that long-range prediction be observed. A lengthy tracking period would better guarantee that future criminal behavior in general and violence in particular for the more dangerous prisoners be given sufficient time to materialize if they are going to. This would be especially vital because a low baserate event is being validated. Determining propensity for violence would be ideally satisfied by establishing lifetime risk for individual prisoners, but this methodological ideal could not be realized for any number of reasons.

Besides being compelled by logic, there also is empirical evidence from early studies of parole outcome encouraging the use of long-term prediction when future risk of violence-prone criminals is being considered. This series of studies (Heilbrun, 1978; Heilbrun & Heilbrun, 1977; Heilbrun, Heilbrun & Heilbrun, 1978; Heilbrun, Knopf & Bruner, 1976) examined whether parole outcome could be predicted from the violent or nonviolent character of the crime that had put the men behind bars. While at least 15 studies prior to the 1976-1978 series had confirmed the greater success of violent criminals on parole relative to nonviolent criminals (see Heilbrun, 1978, for review), this conclusion introduced a seeming paradox. Why should men convicted of violent crimes, known to be more impulsive than property crimes, be better able to demonstrate the self-control that would be required to meet the rigid expectations of parole?

Research in the 1976-1978 series confirmed the success of violent criminals on parole relative to nonviolent offenders when a restricted follow-up period was observed. Given only a few months of tracking, the violent men qualified as safer prospects for conformity to parole conditions and societal laws. These results fell in line with the empirical consensus of prior short-term studies. However, when the criminals were tracked until a final parole determination was made-- either they succeeded and were released from parole or they failed and were returned to prison--a different result was obtained. Violent criminals, whose crimes bring lengthier sentences that result in longer parole terms, turned out to be less successful after they were released. The lesson that I drew from these earlier studies is that if you track people on parole long enough, you find that violent criminals are less capable of adapting their behavior to the expectations of society in general or the criminal justice system in particular. The risk presented by more dangerous men will show itself in the long run.

Given these introductory remarks regarding what constitutes a critical validation study for the dangerousness model. let me return your attention to the study in question. Prediction of future criminal conduct involved tracking periods of 3 years up to 21 years. These figures represent the time from obtaining IQ and personality scale scores used to generate the dangerousness index as part of parole evaluation to the time that the sample was drawn in 1994. All of the men in this study had the opportunity to return to the free world, although the actual amount of time they were free and had an opportunity to recidivate varied from one subject to the next. Time spent out of prison depended upon when parole assessment took place, whether parole was granted immediately or not, and whether the man returned to prison and for how long after committing a new crime. The most apt description of the sampling procedures is that all men in the study were considered in regard to their future criminal conduct, that each had a chance to recidivate following release from prison, and that individuals were tracked variable periods from moderate to very long. Whether the opportunity to recidivate would prove long-term enough to allow the dangerousness model to predict violence as a low baserate event remained to be seen.

Retention in this study from the original criminal subject pool was based upon a clearcut determination of whether new criminal activity had occurred or not.   Only those cases in which nationwide computerized records clearly specified new convictions or the freedom from crime were retained.   Of the 500 criminals with dangerousness scores that made them eligible for tracking, only 248 could be traced and their outcome status unequivocally determined.   These broke down into 155 who were convicted of further crimes, numbering from one new crime following prison release to as many as 17.   A lesser number, 93 men, had remained free of further crimes, either in Georgia or elsewhere, as gauged from the absence of further convictions.

The final sample was comprised predominantly of men whose pre-parole offenses included a crime of violence, a factor of understandable concern to the Parole Board who referred them for evaluation. Accordingly, a violent predisposition, as evidenced by a history of violent crime, could not in itself readily explain differences in dangerous conduct that might be disclosed by the long-term analysis of recidivist and nonrecidivist groups.   If anything, the percentages argue against such an interpretation.   Some 75% of the men who reverted to further crime had a history of criminal violence, yet 87% of the nonrecidivists showed a violent crime in their background.

Analysis of predictive power for the dangerousness index was approached in two ways.   One involved the comparison of recidivism-outcome groups on their dangerousness-index scores, a mode of analysis commonly employed in the research program.   These comparisons addressed the general question of whether the dangerousness score could discriminate at some earlier point in time between groups of criminals whose future conduct would prove them to differ in dangerous criminality.   The analysis of discrimination power was conducted by successive stages in which the least demanding analysis would be completed first and then followed by increasingly difficult discriminations.   An initial comparison between recidivists and nonrecidivists will be presented first.   Multiple recidivists, who reverted to criminal activity more than once during the tracking period, will then be compared to single-offense recidivists and nonrecidivists.   Finally, criminals who engage in violent crime after their release from prison will be examined relative to nonviolent recidivists and nonrecidivists.

The second general approach to testing the power of the dangerousness index was to turn the predictive equation around so that the procedure would be more closely aligned with the requirements of actual individual prediction for the forensic professional.   This addressed the question of how well the dangerousness index score, which would be available prior to prison release, could anticipate the future criminal activity of the prisoner individual. Consideration will be given to the same sequential criteria of predictive validity for the index as described in the preceding paragraph. By introducing the dangerousness score as the independent variable, however, it will be easier to gauge the practical utility of the index as well.

Discrimination Between Recidivism Groups by the Dangerousness Index

The dangerousness index was based upon the multiplicative product of the assessment IQ and Pd-So scores. Raw scores were converted to standard scores with means of 50 and standard deviations of 10 based upon the total sample of 248 criminals. This procedure corresponded to that usually employed throughout the studies reported in this book. After each prisoner was assigned a dangerousness score, he was introduced into the appropriate outcome group depending upon which of the analyses was being conducted.

Comparison of men who recidivate as criminals with men who remain free of crime. The 155 men who reverted to crime after being paroled from prison had obtained an average dangerousness score of 2659.10 prior to their release. This contrasted with the mean score of 2256.50 provided by the nonrecidivist group of 93 men, and statistical test confirmed the significance ($p<.001$) of this difference. Criminals who proved themselves to be more dangerous once they returned to the community by committing new crimes had been portrayed as more dangerous by the index prior to their release from prison.

Comparison of men who commit multiple crimes following release with men who commit one crime and men who remain free of crime. Closer examination of the 155 recidivists in this study revealed that 105 of them had been convicted of more than one crime following release from prison, and the remaining 50 had garnered but one new criminal conviction. The multiple-recidivism group had accumulated an average of 5.41 new convictions on criminal charges over the tracking period covered by this study. The nonrecidivist group from the prior analysis was retained as a standard of comparison for the recidivism groups.

Dangerousness-index score means for the three groups were as follows: multiple recidivists = 2713.48, unitary recidivists = 2544.88, and nonrecidivists = 2256.50. Statistics confirmed the significant variation among these groups (p<.001). Men who committed more than one crime subsequent to their release from incarceration began with higher dangerousness scores than those who showed but one new offense. Both recidivist groups were higher on the psychometric index than the group who did not recidivate.

Comparison of men who commit crimes of violence following release with those committing new nonviolent crimes and men who remain free of crime. The prediction of future violence qualifies as the most critical test of discrimination for the dangerousness model and its quantitative representation by the index score. The extraordinary price paid by the victims of criminal violence places a premium upon identifying those at-risk for such behavior. The crimes committed by 57 men within the tracking period included at least one violent offense, whereas 98 other prisoners engaged in new nonviolent crime(s) following their release from prison. The nonrecidivist group of 93 former convicts remained the same as reported in the previous two analyses of dangerousness. When index averages were determined, wide and significant (p<.001) discrepancies were revealed. Men who were convicted of new violence presented the highest dangerousness scores (M=2973.37). Nonviolent recidivists were intermediate on the index (M=2475.29), and nonrecidivists provided low scores (M=2256.50). The dangerousness index not only successfully discriminated between the violent recidivism, nonviolent recidivism, and crime-free groups as confirmed by statistics, but the index did this so emphatically as to hold out the promise of practical utility.

Length of the tracking period, violent recidivism, and criminal dangerousness. I introduced the methodology of the present study by emphasizing the importance of a long tracking period to disclose with greater certainty who among the men studied would eventually resume their criminal activities. This was deemed to be especially important, since so many prisoners in the sample had a history of violent crime prior to inclusion in this predictive study. Our earlier research had suggested that men proven more dangerous by prior criminal violence were greater risks on parole than nonviolent criminals but only if they were followed for extended periods of time. This concern over length of the tracking period led to one further discrimination analysis as a matter of curiosity. The total sample was split into shorter-term (3-10 years) and longer-term (11-21 years) periods during which criminal activity was monitored. The question is whether the dangerousness score could make the same discrimination between violent recidivists, nonviolent recidivists, and nonrecidivists within both time-frames. If my preliminary concern were justified, I would expect to find clearer discrimination between these groups given the longer tracking period when dangerous men would have had greater opportunity to commit a crime, even to revert to criminal violence.

Results of the more time-focused analysis of violence and dangerousness revealed that the index score discriminated equally well no matter how long the criminals were tracked. Men who were scrutinized over a longer period of time, between 11 and 21 years, presented the predicted order of index scores and significant ($p<.001$) variation: violent recidivists (N=36, M=2868.22); nonviolent recidivists (N=36, M=2370.06); nonrecidivists (N=57, M=2298.81). However, when the shorter tracking period of 3 to 10 years was considered, a significant ($p<.001$) and even more compelling differentiation in averages was found: violent recidivists (N=21, M=3153.62); nonviolent recidivists (N=62, M=2538.00); nonrecidivists (N=36, M=2189.53). It is apparent that my earlier concern about the length of the tracking period was unnecessary as long as the minimum time does not fall below three years. The role of dangerousness in anticipating future violence remains equally clear whether long-term or very long-term periods of observation are allowed.

Past violent and nonviolent criminality and dangerousness -- an examination of false-positive and false-negative errors in terms of future crimes. Even though the dangerousness theory has attracted considerable validating evidence in the studies reported in this book, I have attempted to portray these results in a conservative way. The theory, or at least the dangerousness index, has not been in line with criminal conduct in every case; being valid does not require that a psychological theory have universal applicability. Other explanations of criminality are doubtless going to be more relevant in some cases. In addition, the dangerousness theory is not completely articulated at this point in time nor is the two-factor quantitative index fully representative of the theory as it stands. Furthermore, the index is a working psychometric tool and certainly loses something in translation from the behavioral phenomena it represents.

I have once again reviewed the limiting features of the model and index in order to make just the opposite point. Some of the limitations that are suggested by the research data may be more apparent than real, and the power of the dangerousness model might be even greater than I have made out. The clearest case in point harkens back to the first validity evidence we considered, several chapters ago. There the dangerousness scores of men who had committed a violent crime were compared with those of other men who had only a nonviolent criminal history. The theoretical model called for greater dangerousness in the violent criminals and two bodies of data confirmed this expectation statistically. However, the discrimination was more difficult than I had expected. Some violent criminals had lower dangerousness scores than their crimes seem to call for, whereas other nonviolent criminals presented higher index scores and a level of dangerousness not evident in their property crimes. Using the lexicon of predictive accuracy, these represent false-negative errors for the index (called low dangerous by index but shown to be high dangerous by prior violent crime) and false-positive errors (called high dangerous by index but shown to be low dangerous by prior nonviolent crime).

It was pointed out earlier in the book that these false-negative and false-positive cases may not be errors at all but rather a matter of timing or explanatory relevance of the theoretical model. I placed special emphasis upon the false-positive index scores of nonviolent criminals and have already offered some evidence on whether high dangerousness scores for less dangerous nonviolent criminals are necessarily erroneous. One could reason this way. Some very dangerous criminals as far as psychological risk is concerned may have not as yet encountered the circumstances of planning or conducting a crime where their cognitive limitations would be conducive to victim harm. Collaborative crime in which dangerous criminals would be required to take less responsibility for planning and conduct would be an example. Their danger to others, especially the risk of violence, lies ahead.

I could offer what I consider an equally compelling argument regarding why some violent criminals are accurately described as low in dangerousness by model specifications. Perhaps their violence is better explained from another psychological perspective or lacks intent. In either case, the low dangerousness score (and what seems to be a false-negative error) might accurately signal less risk to victims in the years ahead. Instead of having failed to detect the dangerous qualities of the violent offender, the low index score could be taken as a harbinger of a more benign criminal future.

The long-term prediction data offer a prime opportunity to examine my proposals regarding false-negative and false-positive discrimination errors. Rather than allowing the issues to remain speculative, prospective evidence can put the proposals to a test; if something is not supposed to happen or is supposed to happen in the future, the projections can be verified. I will start by considering violent criminals for whom the index seemed to misfire. Men who were incarcerated for committing a violent crime at the time the dangerousness scores were determined fell into one of three groups based upon their criminal record during the post-release tracking period. One group was responsible for another violent crime thereby confirming their proneness to violence (N=48); this violence-violence category includes those who are clearly very dangerous in their criminal conduct. A second group was made up of violent criminals who reverted to nonviolent crime during the follow-up period (N=68); as nonviolent recidivists they were considered to be at an intermediate level of risk to the victims of their eventual crimes. The third group of violent criminals remained free of crime over the protracted period (N=80); they will be designated as the low-risk group despite their early violence.

In order to substantiate my proposal that low index scores for violent criminals could represent valid descriptors of victim risk despite the appearance of error, I would have to find a marked discrepancy in dangerousness between the high index scores of the violent-violent criminals and the low index scores of the violent-nonrecidivist criminals. The violent men who turned to nonviolent crime should assume intermediate index status. That pattern of dangerousness is precisely what was found. The dangerousness-index mean for the men who repeated their violence (M=2969.38) departed dramatically from the average index score for violent criminals who stayed free of crime during the tracking period (M=2250.55). The men who followed their original violence with only nonviolent offenses had an average index score that fell in-between (M=2431.13), and the variation among these means was highly significant (p<.001). Lower dangerousness scores for men guilty of violent crime did not represent measurement error when considered collectively. Rather, these low scores were predictive of future conduct that involved much less risk to the victims of crime then would have been anticipated based upon prior violence.

The false-positive case in which high dangerousness scores are found for criminals who have been convicted of only property crimes at the time of measurement was analyzed in much the same way. Discussion of this analysis, presented earlier in the book, bears repetition. The most dangerous group as far as their future conduct was concerned included nonviolent criminals who ended up committing a violent crime after release from prison (N=9). An intermediate category was made up of nonviolent criminals who were responsible for future nonviolent crimes (N=30). Ranking as least dangerous were nonviolent offenders who were crime-free during the tracking period (N=13). The validity of dangerousness scores would lead us to expect a high average for those criminals who proved to be violent given enough time and a low average for the nonrecidivists. Those who continued to engage in property crimes should display an intermediate index mean.

Again, the results confirmed the predictive value of the index whether it had originally appeared out of line with criminal history or not. Nonviolent criminals who turned violent had been designated as very dangerous by index score (M=2995.11); nonviolent men who persisted in nonviolent crime were considerably less dangerous (M=2457.63); nonviolent offenders who did not engage in further crime qualified as least dangerous (M=2293.15). These differences (p<.001) testify to the legitimacy of my proposal regarding false-positive errors. If high dangerousness scores are obtained, they warrant concern whether the man has displayed criminal violence to that point in his life or is still considered a nonviolent offender.

One further observation seems warranted before I conclude this section on seeming false-negative and false-positive measurement errors by the dangerousness-index score. The analyses that I called upon to examine issues of error have added theoretical value, because they affirm the usefulness of both high and low dangerousness scores in measuring criminal risk. There has been an emphasis on high index scores and dangerous outcomes in the validity evidence throughout the book. The results that we have just covered include good evidence that low index scores can be used to predict less dangerous criminal outcomes in the future and even a crime-free adjustment. That this evidence was generated in part from analysis of violent offenders qualifies as especially worthy of note. The data run counter to one of the most basic principles of prediction in psychology. Peoples' future behavior should conform to what they have done in the past -- unless they are violent criminals with low dangerousness scores!

Prediction of Recidivism from the Dangerousness Index

I prefer comparing the dangerousness scores of discrete criminal-outcome groups as a validating procedure for the theoretical model in that it allows more powerful statistical tests based upon continuous scores to be employed. There is something to be said for examining the relationship from the other direction, however, since it allows me to shift the emphasis from scientific validation of theory to considering the pragmatic qualities of the index. In the context of the present predictive evidence, this would mean that the emphasis would shift from validity of the theoretical model to how well the index will work if it is used in the individual case to anticipate future criminal conduct. In professional circumstances a dangerousness score for a specific prisoner should prove useful if it not only provided a prediction of his future criminal conduct but allowed a sense of the odds that the prediction will be on the mark. In this section I will explore how well the index score could have predicted the various recidivism outcomes.

Prediction of recidivism and nonrecidivism from the dangerousness index. The procedure for examining predictions from the dangerousness index to dichotomous recidivism outcomes began by breaking the index score distribution for the entire sample down into four quartiles. Roughly the highest 25% of the scores became the high-dangerousness group, and the remaining three quartiles of scores defined high-intermediate, low-intermediate, and low dangerousness. The score ranges defining these levels of dangerousness were: high >2910; high intermediate, 2400-2910; low intermediate, 1932-2399; low, <1932. The analysis of prediction proceeded by determining the likelihood that specified recidivism outcomes could have been forecast given scores falling at each level of dangerousness.

The top section of Table 16 includes the number of men at each dangerousness level who either committed a new crime or who did not. These frequencies were found to be disproportional using a nonparametric statistical test ($p<.001$). Prisoners obtaining dangerousness scores above 2910 (top quartile) were almost five times more likely to be recidivists than nonrecidivists. Scores falling in the third and second quartiles were associated with a moderately better chance than not of committing another crime, whereas scorers in the bottom quartile of dangerousness scores were slightly more likely to be nonrecidivists. Considering that the entire sample of prisoners for

Table 16: Frequencies for Various Recidivism Outcome Groups at Four Levels of Dangerousness Scores

| Recidivism Outcome Group | Levels of Dangerousness by Model Scores | | | |
	High	High Intermediate	Low Intermediate	Low
Recidivist	52	36	38	29
Nonrecidivist	11	27	23	32
Multiple Recidivist	37	24	28	16
Single Recidivist	15	12	10	13
Nonrecidivist	11	27	23	32
Violent Recidivist	28	13	10	6
Nonviolent Recidivist	24	23	28	23
Nonrecidivist	11	27	23	32

whom future criminal conduct could be authenticated had a baserate for recidivism that exceeded 62%, bringing the rate of repeat crime down to 48% by requiring scores of 1931 or less is not without merit. Nevertheless, the major contribution of the index score in long-term prediction of criminal recidivism was shown by this analysis to be at the upper end of the dimension.

Prediction of multiple recidivism, one-time recidivism, and nonrecidivism. The middle section of Table 16 presents frequency data relevant to the prediction of multiple and single-crime recidivism along with nonrecidivism at the four quartile levels of dangerousness. An overall test of the frequency data was significant ($p<.001$). Closer examination reveals that the most dangerous men (>2910) were convicted of more than one crime in 59% of the cases, 30% received one new conviction, and only 17% avoided further criminality. At the other extreme, when dangerousness scores fell below 1932, a very different picture emerged. About 26% received multiple convictions, 21% recidivated but once, and 52% remained free of crime. The middle two quartiles of index scorers again looked much alike with both sets of prisoners providing recidivism results falling in-between those of the quartile extremes.

The conclusion that seems most apparent in these findings, beyond the fact that future crime can be predicted, is that multiple recidivists are going to be concentrated in the top quartile of dangerousness scores and nonrecidivists are going to be represented predominantly in the bottom quartile. The extremes of future criminality in the frequency sense are to be predicted by the extremes of index scores.

Prediction of violent recidivism, nonviolent recidivism, and nonrecidivism. Table 16 (bottom section) includes the frequencies of outcome for violent and nonviolent recidivism, along with nonrecidivism, for the four dangerousness quartiles. Overall statistical confirmation of proportional variation was found ($p<.001$). About 44% of the men whose dangerousness scores fell in the top quartile committed new violent offenses, while 38% were nonviolent recidivists. Only 17% remain crime-free. Within the lowest quartile, only 10% perpetrated a violent crime, 38% recidivated by nonviolent crime, and 52% were nonrecidivists. As expected, the middle quartiles of dangerousness scorers provided outcome findings that were intermediate to those of the extremes. The prevalence of violent recidivism in these similar-appearing intermediate groups was much more like that found in the lowest quartile, however.

Two related observations seem worthy of note given the prediction rates presented in the bottom section of Table 16. The dangerousness score did not fare well in predicting nonviolent crime for this particular sample. The rates of nonviolent recidivism were much the same at each level of dangerousness. However, the extremes of victim risk, violent harm and freedom from crime, proved to be amenable to prediction. Violent crime, previously held to be the bane of criminal prediction, was commonly observed in the high-dangerousness group and rarely observed in the low-dangerousness group. Freedom from further crime also was predictable, especially at the quartile extremes. Long-term prediction, as it might be required of a forensic professional, worked fairly well as long as the dangerousness index was used in its higher and lower ranges and harm to the victims of crime was considered at the extremes of violence or nothing. Increased power of the dangerousness model, that should follow further theoretical development, should alleviate these gaps in prediction.

General Conclusion

The results of this investigation complete my presentation of evidence supporting the validity of the dangerousness model and pave the way for consideration of issues confronted in developing the theoretical model that will follow. The accumulation of empirical data produced by the many studies of discrimination, prediction, and correlates relevant to the dangerousness model may actually seem like overkill, although it is hard to imagine that too much evidence can be brought to bear when a new theory of criminality and violence is proposed. At least with this much evidence, serious challenge to the theory should involve some alternative explanation for the substantial number of scientific findings that would otherwise be left unexplained.

Section III

Issues Related to the Theoretical Modeling

of Criminal Dangerousness

CHAPTER 8

Dangerousness and Race

Construction of a new theoretical model of criminal dangerousness to help explain the occurrence of crime in general and violent actions in particular and its validation through programmatic research have been considered in the previous sections of this book. The two-factor proposal involving the dangers of concomitant antisociality and flawed cognitive/social attributes has attracted a considerable amount of empirical support as it stands. Nevertheless, I am left with one further goal in developing the model to its fullest with the evidence in hand. The limitations of the model at this point in time will have much to do with psychological factors that have yet to be identified but may be important for explaining crime and violence. Some of these new determinants will certainly have to do with breadth of applicability, the range of people for whom the model is relevant.

In the chapters of this section I shall examine three important human demographics -- race, gender, and presence of mental disorder -- as they may influence model applicability. Does the two-factor model help explain criminality and violence in both black and white offenders?; in both women and men?; in those who are mentally ill and those who are not? The demographics of race, gender, and mental disorder represent interactive features that could run the gamut of importance. The model could prove to be so inapplicable when extended across any of these categorical lines as to require distinct theoretical models. At the other extreme, theoretical fit could be so close across demographic categories that the same model would be retained but for an expanded population of criminals.

The theoretical issue of race, criminal dangerousness, and victim harm to be covered in this chapter, was considered only in terms of black/white disparities in criminals or in criminal-victim patterns. This represented the only feasible racial inquiry that was available given the geographic locale of the research. Blacks make up a substantial proportion of the prison population in Georgia, and a black/white racial analysis was both relevant and feasible. Criminals having hispanic or oriental racial origins were rarely encountered.

Two procedures will be followed in order to establish whether race influences the applicability of the dangerousness model. The first procedure followed from the fact that all of our criminal samples included substantial numbers of subjects distinguishable by race. This made it possible to reanalyze the data already reported to you in the validity chapters to determine whether the results for each sample were representative of both racial groups. I did not reanalyze every sample of reported data, since it became obvious after several efforts that the same pattern of results was consistently forthcoming.

The second way in which racial disparities in dangerousness were evaluated involved the more complex consideration of racial identity for both the criminal and victim involved in a given crime. An association between dangerousness of the criminal and the intraracial (black-on-black, white-on-white) or interracial (black-on-white, white-on-black) nature of transactional crime had been studied originally in an investigation of death-sentence verdicts in Georgia (Heilbrun, Foster, & Golden, 1989). This research posed an alternative way of understanding the undeniable role of race in murder sentences by introducing the construct of criminal dangerousness. The study also raised new questions about the way dangerousness, race of the criminal, and victim race may interact. Given impetus by the findings in the case of murder, further sampling was conducted for purposes of this book that allowed for examination of intraracial/interracial criminal transaction with the victim of rape and its relationship to dangerousness.

The studies of criminals and criminal-victim patterns, described in fuller detail on subsequent pages, will help answer several questions relating to dangerousness and race. Does the dangerousness model apply equally well to black and white criminals? Is there a difference in the dangerousness and risk of even more serious harm posed by the violent criminal who targets someone of a different race relative to the man whose violence is directed toward a victim of the same race? Do the implications regarding dangerousness and criminal/victim race patterns hold true for both the white and black criminal?

Reanalysis of Previously Reported Evidence Regarding Dangerousness in Terms of Race

Violent versus nonviolent criminals. Evidence considered earlier demonstrated higher dangerousness scores for men who had committed violent crimes when compared with nonviolent criminals. Reexamination of this relationship using discrete racial categories for the criminals provided the dangerousness figures reported in Table 17. Statistics revealed but one significant effect. Violent criminals were more dangerous than nonviolent criminals ($p<.01$), and this was true whether the crimes were perpetrated by either white or black offenders. In statistical terms, a main (general) effect of criminal category was found without an accompanying interaction between category and race. This statistical pattern, a main effect without an interaction, will be used in all analyses to be reported in this section to infer that the relationship under consideration does not differ for black and white criminals.

Sex-offenders. A number of the variables regarded as criteria of dangerousness were reanalyzed for a contact sex-offender sample after regrouping by criterion status and race of the criminal. Table 18 lists the dangerousness scores for the various groups generated by these procedures. The four sets of statistical analyses provided identical results with regard to white and black sex-offenders. Men whose sex-offenses were directed against adults were more dangerous than child molesters ($p<.01$), intoxicated men were more dangerous than those not intoxicated during the sex-offense ($p<.001$), repeat sex-offenders were more dangerous than nonrecidivists ($p<.005$), and sex-offenders who had problems on parole were more dangerous than men who did not ($p<.005$). All of these effects were found without interaction with race of the criminal.

Penalty for murder. Prior investigation disclosed that men who receive the death penalty following conviction for murder in Georgia are more dangerous than men who receive life sentences for the same offense. A further breakdown of this finding by race of the murderer provided the results found in Table 19. Again we find a general effect without interaction by race. Men who receive the death sentence for murder are more dangerous than those who are given life sentences ($p<.001$) whether they are black or white.

Prison misconduct. When prison misconduct for prisoners of both races was determined within three levels of dangerousness, the

Table 17:   Dangerousness as Related to Violence or Nonviolence of Crime and Race of Criminal

		Race of Criminal		
	White		Black	
Nature of Crime	N	M	N	M
Violent	76	2518.55	56	2649.89
Nonviolent	76	2198.42	29	2384.28

Table 18: Dangerousness of Various Criterion Groups Associated with Sex-offenses for White and Black Sex-offenders

	Race of Criminal			
	White		Black	
Criterion Group	N	M	N	M
Age of Victim				
Child	157	2217.50	53	2645.70
Adult	23	2449.65	47	2973.77
Intoxicated During Sex-offense				
Intoxicated	76	2448.29	51	2913.14
Not Intoxicated	95	2086.46	43	2561.02
Recidivism in Sex-offense				
Recidivist	51	2473.22	21	3299.95
Nonrecidivist	124	2163.21	80	2688.44
Parole Outcome				
More Successful	136	2154.46	44	2726.73
Less Successful	45	2600.44	49	2872.80

Table 19: Dangerousness of White and Black Murderers Given the Death Penalty and Life Sentences

| | Race of Criminal | | | |
| | White | | Black | |
Sentence	N	M	N	M
Death Penalty	41	2393.07	44	2953.70
Life in Prison	61	2185.48	65	2525.40

results reported in Table 20 were found. The single effect disclosed by statistics involved levels of dangerousness. The most dangerous men in the upper third of index scores were involved in singularly serious misconduct (p<.05) whether white or black inmates were being considered. There was no statistical interaction; similar curvilinearity of misconduct scores was observed across dangerousness levels for both races.

Characteristics of the crime. Looking back at the degree of brutality involved in the act of rape with race of the criminal in mind, I again found that the overall effect of dangerousness could be detected within both of the racially homogenous groups. The white rapists who had committed more brutal sexual assaults presented higher dangerousness scores (M = 2383.38) than did the white rapists whose crimes were lower in rated brutality (M = 2178.28). Directing attention to black rapists, higher brutality ratings were associated with greater dangerousness (M = 2687.89) than were lower brutality ratings (M = 2377.61). Statistics revealed an overall relation between brutality of sexual assault and dangerousness (p<.05) with no distinction by race of the rapist (no interaction).

Socio-economic class. Although an analysis of social class membership and dangerousness of the criminal was not reported earlier in the book, I can take advantage of these analyses by race to provide that information. The Georgia correctional system divides social class into three levels -- lower, middle, and upper -- based essentially on indicators of material wealth. It will come as no surprise that the samples of prisoners collected for our studies drew heavily from the lower class with some lesser representation of middle-class criminals. Upper-class prisoners were not encountered. The sample that was examined with regard to socio-economic class, race, and dangerousness included only sex-offenders and broke down into 70% lower class and 30% middle class.

Middle-class sex-offenders who were white provided low dangerousness scores (N = 67, M = 2069.81) when compared with lower-class white sex-offenders (N = 108, M = 2472.70). Similarly, middle-class black sex-offenders presented lower dangerousness scores (N = 14, M = 2550.78) than their lower-class counterparts (N = 83, M = 2922.80). The relationship of social class to dangerousness was significant overall (p<.05), and there was no interaction of race and social class.

Table 20: Dangerousness of Black and White Prison Inmates and Prison Misconduct

Level of Dangerousness	Race of Prisoner			
	White		Black	
	N	M	N	M
High	43	8.67	24	12.46
Intermediate	45	4.73	22	6.91
Low	52	3.69	14	7.21

Conclusions from reanalyses. The evidence reported thus far should make the point that the dangerousness model is applicable across race of the criminal. All nine relationships that were initially chosen for examination held up for the white and black criminal alike, so further reanalyses appeared to be unnecessary. There is another recurring feature of the racial comparisons upon which I have reserved comment, although the reader may well have noticed. Black criminals, considered as a group, were consistently higher on the index score than white criminals; more often than not the racial difference was reliable. Accordingly, while the relationships between a number of criteria and correlates of dangerous criminal behavior and model-defined dangerousness were the same for both races, black criminals emerged as more dangerous than white criminals based upon the same theoretical model.

I see nothing obvious to suggest that the overall higher dangerousness scores for black criminals are artifacts of our research procedures. The IQ test was developed to be relatively free of cultural bias and is used by the state of Georgia with that in mind. The antisociality variable contributed to higher black index scores whether personality questionnaire scales or social history data were used. Personality tests have been accused of being more appropriate for whites, although the case that they are inappropriate for blacks has not been made. However, social-history information taken from a prisoner's file should be free of bias. We will return to this issue of racial differences in degree of dangerousness in the forthcoming section when the racial identity of both the criminal and the victim are considered.

Race of Criminal and Victim in Violent Crimes and Dangerousness

Race of criminal and race of victim as related to the dangerousness of murderers. Heilbrun, Foster, and Golden (1989) explored the interactive role of criminal and victim race in violent crime. Our interest was generated by the results of a study conducted by Baldus, Pulaski, and Woodworth (1983) which challenged the Georgia sentencing procedures in assignment of the death penalty for murder. Although the background for our study bearing upon a controversy over alleged racial prejudice in the Georgia courts goes beyond the topic of racial patterns in violent crime and dangerousness, the reader might be interested in why the evidence was collected in the first place.

Baldus and his co-investigators reported different death-penalty rates in cases of murder during the 1970s depending upon the particular combination of criminal-victim race. The death penalty (rather than life in prison) was imposed for 22% of the blacks who killed whites, 8% of the whites who killed whites, 1%of the blacks who killed blacks, and 3% of the whites who killed blacks. These disparities in sentencing led Baldus and his group to assume racial bias against blacks in the criminal justice system when the murder victim was white. It could be reasoned that bias resulted from two prejudicial assumptions by the courts. Greater value could have been placed upon the life of a white victim, thereby justifying more severe punishment for anyone who takes a white life. Coupled with this, the black's place in the southern social order could continue to result in especially severe punishment for crossing racial lines and killing a white.

The possibility that there might be an explanation other than bias for the disproportionality of the death sentence in black-on-white murder convictions in Georgia was slow to be recognized following the 1983 Baldus paper. The U.S. Supreme Court heard a case in 1986 (Supreme Court of the United States, 1987) in which the petitioner, a black man who had killed a white victim, alleged discrimination in his death sentence based upon the disproportionality of execution verdicts in Georgia given that racial circumstance. The Baldus data served as the basis for the petition. Even though the Court ruled by majority against the petition, they did so without challenging the racial bias implied by the data. The majority decision resulted instead from the lack of evidence that racial considerations had been instrumental in the specific case of the petitioner, although by implication prejudicial sentencing was assumed in the general case. Opinions of dissenting justices were less restrained, expressing continuing concern over the racial bias in Georgia's death-penalty procedures. This minority entertained no doubts regarding the meaning of the sentencing disproportionalities in the Baldus evidence.

The first public challenge to the assumption of bias within the Georgia death-penalty findings, to my knowledge at least, was raised by Katz (1987). An Atlanta newspaper carried the testimony he had given about four years earlier in federal court that disputed the allegations of prejudice by the Baldus group and supported the credibility of the Georgia sentencing procedures. He noted that homicide cases involving white victims, upon closer examination, were more heinous than cases in which the victim was black. White-victim cases were:

"... much more likely to involve other offenses, such as armed robbery, kidnapping, or rape. They were more likely to be brutal, with higher rates of mutilation, torture, and clubbing or stomping the victim to death. And they were more likely to be cold-blooded, with the assailant motivated, for example, by the pursuit of money or the necessity to silence a witness to a crime."

Katz's case examination revealed that black homicides claiming black victims were more likely to include mitigating factors. Many were instigated by domestic arguments, fights over drugs, and quarrels with friends -- frequently they resulted in surrender to authorities and remorse. Katz, then, explained the higher percentage of death-penalty sentences in cases where a black killed a white largely in terms of the absence of mitigating circumstances in interracial murder. The same lack of mitigation would prevail in the opposite interracial case in which a white murdered a black victim. However, Katz found this racial pattern to be so rare that the lack of mitigation in such cases failed to inflate the death-penalty rate for white murderers as it had for black murderers.

Our own investigation of the role of race in the Georgia sentencing procedures following conviction for murder (Heilbrun, Foster, & Golden, 1989) began shortly before the delayed publication of the Katz testimony in the Atlanta newspaper. Katz had emphasized the relative absence of mitigating circumstances in his review of the Baldus cases involving black murderers and white victims. We had observed a complementary trend in the same evidence. The number of statutory aggravating factors in death-penalty cases involving white victims exceeded the number in cases where blacks were victimized and the same severe punishment was exacted. This difference in count simply quantifies the Katz observation that murders of white victims involved more heinous circumstances than when the victims were black.

Our interest in the Baldus evidence and what seemed like its unchallenged interpretation was that criminal dangerousness seemed to provide a straightforward alternative conclusion to courtroom bias. Blacks who kill white victims receive the death penalty more frequently, because they have committed more malicious crimes as evidenced by an excess of aggravating circumstances. More malicious violence would be found in more dangerous criminals. Taken to an alternative conclusion, black murderers of white victims were more frequently sentenced to die, because their dangerousness had promoted more heinous murders.

A skeptic could still maintain, given both the observed discrepancy in aggravating and mitigating factors, that bias was still operative in the investigation or adjudication of a white murder, especially if the person suspected or accused of the crime was black. What represents aggravation or mitigation and the weight assigned to these factors as far as the death penalty is concerned are conceivably subject to bias themselves. Some new approach was needed to disentangle bias and more heinous criminal conduct in explaining disproportionate death-sentencing of blacks killing whites. We believed that the dangerousness model provided it, since it allowed the focus of investigation to be shifted away from unverifiable bias as the basis for courtroom decisions. If the black-on-white murderer scheduled for execution is more dangerous, there is independent evidence explaining malicious violent conduct. Disproportionate death sentences for black men who kill white victims can be understood in terms of the psychological characteristics of the murderers, not their racial origins.

The Heilbrun, Foster, and Golden sample of 243 men found guilty of murder included 109 who had received the death penalty after 1973 and were still awaiting execution on death row at the time the data were collected in 1987. The death-penalty murderers were made up of 55 whites and 54 blacks and represented a complete sampling except for a few whose files were unavailable. Random selection availed us of 134 murderers, 63 whites and 71 blacks, who were serving a life sentence in prison. Analysis of criminal-victim racial patterns and sentencing outcome was curtailed by the fact that our search turned up only 4 out of the 118 cases of convicted white murderers in which the victim was black. As Katz observed earlier regarding Georgia crime, the situation in which a white murders a black victim is exceedingly rare. Accordingly, I cannot provide a complete analysis of racial patterns and dangerousness from the Heilbrun, Foster, and Golden data. Instead, I will concentrate upon cases involving white victims only, varying race of the murderer and the severity of sentencing. These crimes will include the critical cases in which black murderers victimized whites and were subject to presumed bias in the form of the death penalty.

Table 21 includes the dangerousness scores for black and white

Table 21: Dangerousness of White and Black Murderers Receiving the Death Penalty or Life Sentence for Killing a White Victim

Sentence	Race of Criminal			
	White		Black	
	N	M	N	M
Death Penalty	39	2369.08	23	2853.74
Life in Prison	51	2081.65	15	2627.13

murderers who received the death sentence or a sentence of life in prison following conviction for killing a white victim. As can be seen, greater dangerousness of men receiving the death sentence can be found for both white and black murderers who have killed white victims. This difference from life-sentence murderers, confirmed statistically (p<.05), aligns greater dangerousness and excesses of aggravating circumstances associated with death-penalty murders of white victims noted earlier. Black-on-white murderers who received the death penalty were the most dangerous of the racial subsets (M=2853.74) using index scores as a gauge. This is especially evident when you compare them to their counterparts in crime, the white murderer of a white victim who was sentenced to die for his crime (M=2369.08, p<.001).

The more extreme dangerousness of black murderers who have killed white victims and received the death penalty allows for two conclusions. Returning to the prejudice issue addressed by the 1989 study, there is no compelling reason to invoke racial bias in sentencing to explain why black murderers are more likely to be given a death penalty than white murderers in cases where the victim is white. The black-on-white murderer may not only lack the relationship with his victim that allows for mitigation of the crime, as Katz has observed, but he also qualifies as more dangerous and thus more at-risk for the excesses of harm that results in aggravated criminal circumstances. The second conclusion returns us to the role of racial patterning and dangerousness in violent crime. Race does seem to be an important consideration as far as explaining the most heinous form of violence by dangerousness of the criminal. Blacks who murder whites present a level of dangerousness consistent with a verdict of execution.

We also collected supplementary information regarding criminal circumstances that we hoped would cast additional light on the dangerousness findings whatever they might be. For the most part, this information went unreported in the 1989 journal article due to space limitations. These supplementary data are worth our time, since they do bring issues relating to race, dangerousness, and punishment into sharper focus. One of the vital observations provided by Katz in his testimony regarding the death sentence in Georgia -- blacks killing whites typically have had little or no previous relationship with their victims -- was subjected to quantitative analysis. Information in the prisoner's file allowed us to establish which of the following relationships existed between criminal and victim: stranger (=1), acquaintance (=2), friend (=3), and original or marital family (=4).

When blacks killed blacks, the murderer was relatively familiar with his victim whether the death penalty ($\underline{M}$ = 2.61) or a life sentence ($\underline{M}$ = 2.79) was invoked; on average, the relationship fell closer to friend than acquaintance.   When blacks murdered whites, they were relative strangers. Again this was the case whether a life sentence ($\underline{M}$ = 1.25) or a death penalty ($\underline{M}$ = 1.25) resulted from the crime; both averages fell close to describing a total stranger.   A similar comparison of intraracial and interracial killings for white murderers was not possible because too few white-on-black cases were found. These data confirm Katz's contention that blacks typically murder white victims who are strangers with diminished likelihood of mitigating circumstances.

Further analysis of the criminal circumstances focused exclusively upon cases involving the slaying of a white victim that resulted in the death penalty. Two aspects of the crime were considered -- the verbal and physical resistance offered by the victims prior to their deaths and the cruelty involved in the murder. The reader may recall that these two variables, considered in combination, helped to explain the role of dangerousness in the violence of rape. All rapists (without regard to race or dangerousness) tend to subject women to more brutal treatment if they resist their sexual aggression. It was the highly dangerous rapist, however, who was found to be brutal (to some lesser extent) even when the victim offered little or no resistance. Cruelty without provocation served as a hallmark of the dangerous rapist. These earlier findings encouraged an analysis of resistance and cruelty in murder to determine whether the same hallmark of dangerousness would be found in the murder of whites that bring the death penalty. Specifically, would this malevolent pattern be equally apparent in black and white murderers of white victims in death-penalty cases?

Two forms of resistance were rated from the description of criminal circumstances -- verbal resistance such as protest or threat and physical resistance to the criminal's advances. Each was rated on an 8-point scale, and the two ratings were added for a resistance score. The second variable, cruelty of the homicide, was rated on a 5-point scale in which higher scores indicated a more heinous killing and more suffering for the victim. This variable represents one of the prominent circumstances that allows for the death penalty. The information necessary for generating one type of rating or the other was not always available in the file, so some criminals had to be dropped for a particular analysis.

The total number of black and white men who had claimed a

white victim and received the death penalty were split at the median resistance offered by the victim. The degree of cruelty involved in the killing as well as the dangerousness of the killer were then determined for the white and black murderers who were met by greater and less resistance. Table 22 includes the average figures for these groups and variables. Statistical analysis of these findings provided an interaction effect for both cruelty ($p<.05$) and dangerousness ($p<.001$).

Table 22 findings for black men who murder white victims and are given a death sentence indicate that a high level of cruelty was observed only when the victim offered relatively little resistance. This was the case for a majority of the black-on-white killings (61%). When the dangerousness of the black murderer was calculated, those who showed the more malicious behavior without facing serious resistance from the victim were singularly dangerous criminals ($M=3044.54$). Thus, we can see that excessive dangerousness in black murderers of white victims is associated with criminal circumstances that are not only consistent with the assignment of the death penalty but might even encourage it. The more brutal treatment of a victim who is offering little resistance seems to invite more severe punishment. These findings are also in line with the earlier analysis of cruelty and resistance in rape that showed more dangerous criminals to be a special risk to women who do little to resist the rapist. Racial patterns of criminal and victim were not reported, although we will get to that later in this chapter.

White death-penalty murderers of white victims presented totally dissimilar results. No relationship appeared between the brutality involved in the murders and the resistance provided by the victims. The murders were rated as very cruel whether the victim resisted strongly or not. Furthermore, higher dangerousness was found among those white murderers who met greater opposition, not less opposition. The question remains how this very embedded set of racial differences is to be explained.

Given the small numbers of criminals that were left for analysis, considerable caution is due; nevertheless, there is at least a partial explanation to be found for the disparate results if victim gender is considered. About 60% of the white victims of death-penalty white murderers were women, and only 31% of the victims were female in the case of black murderers. The rated cruelty involved in murdering white women was higher ($M=4.44$) for criminals of both races than was true when white males were victims ($M=3.17$, $p<.05$). Since we know

Table 22: Cruelty of the Murders and Dangerousness of Black and White Death-penalty Murderers as a Function of Resistance Offered by the White Victims

	Race of the Murderer							
	Black				White			
Crime-related	Higher Victim Resistance		Lower Victim Resistance		Higher Victim Resistance		Lower Victim Resistance	
Variable	N	M	N	M	N	M	N	M
Cruelty of the Murder	12	2.16	19	3.90	17	4.06	16	3.75
Dangerousness of the Murderer	7	2603.43	11	3044.54	15	2417.47	10	1837.00

NOTE: *The discrepancy in numbers for the groups involved in the figures on cruelty and dangerousness stems from inconsistent availability of information in the criminal files.*

from previous analysis that the killer and victim are likely known to each other in white intraracial murder, we can surmise that domestic violence played a large part and that the cruelty toward the woman frequently evolved when emotions overwhelmed the man's cognitive controls. Perhaps the loss of control within especially emotional domestic disputes might be enough to explain the cruel manner in which women are killed without regard to the measured dangerousness of the murderer. This cannot be relevant to black murderers, however, since far fewer female victims were claimed, and the racial disparity between murderer and victim makes domestic violence a less likely circumstance.

Rather than depending upon emotional compromise of cognitive control in the brutal slaying of familiar women that was proposed as a major dynamic for white death-penalty murderers, the black counterpart case must take into consideration that the white victim is likely to be a man and a stranger. Given those demographics, we are left with the further observation that greater cruelty is going to accompany less resistance to being victimized. Two possibilities can be suggested. The cognitive limitations of the very dangerous black criminal may lead him to misrepresent the reactions of the white victim so that he perceives resistance when none is intended. Recall that the black murderer in this circumstance had an index score over 3000 on average. Cognitive limitations at that level could certainly allow for misrepresentation of victim intentions. Alternatively, the black murderer who is that dangerous might carry an antipathy toward whites into the criminal situation and gain satisfaction from tormenting a more helpless white victim. Such racial animosity could be considered a derivative of high antisociality or cognitive flaw in the 3000-plus criminal.

Race of criminal and race of victim as related to the dangerousness of rapists. The examination of dangerousness for white and black murderers in terms of severity of sentencing was made more difficult by the emergence of interactive variables that seemed important in understanding relationships between criminal/victim racial patterns and dangerousness. Whites did not murder blacks in enough cases to allow for study. Women-as-victims was an important factor for white murderers but not black, and familiarity of the victim depended upon the racial pattern. Cruelty of the murder, which would be an important consideration for imposing the death penalty, assumed a very different relationship to white victim resistance for the two races and aligned differently with dangerousness. While these findings alerted us to racial differences in violent conduct if victim race is considered, the complications invited a second look at the issue.

My choice for a second analysis was another violent crime in which the race of both the criminal and the victim would be important but for which gender of the victim would not represent a complicating factor -- rape. Unfortunately, the new study did involve the same sampling limitation that was evident in the investigation of homicides; interracial rapes involving a white rapist and a black woman victim were too infrequently encountered to include that pattern in the new study. I ended up doing much the same kind of analysis as in the previous study of racial patterns in death-penalty murder convictions. Primary comparisons were made between white and black rapists who had victimized white women. Black-on-black rapes were considered for whatever added information might result.

Two samples of men who had been convicted of rape, aggravated rape, or rape/sodomy as their most recent offenses were drawn for this analysis. Interestingly enough, examination of the sentences handed down by the courts for these crimes suggested the same bias that was so widely heralded in assigning the death penalty for murder. If the highly-variable punishment (low of five years to a high of life in prison) is broken down by the racial composition of rapist and victim, the more severe punishment accorded a black man raping a white woman becomes obvious. Table 23 reports the frequencies within both samples that three levels of punishment were handed down following conviction for interracial and intraracial rape. A tripartite division by sentencing severity was determined independently for each sample (see footnote to Table 23).

The frequency data in Table 23 displayed significant variation. In sample 1 (which was used only for this sentencing analysis), black men who raped white women more frequently received severe sentences than was true for white men who raped white women and black men who raped black women ($p<.01$). The findings for Sample 2 were the same ($p<.05$); black men convicted of raping a white woman were more severely punished than either set of intraracial rapists. Should this be construed as evidence that the black man is treated more harshly in southern courts if he has crossed racial boundaries by sexual aggression toward a white woman? It depends, in my way of thinking at least, upon whether an alternative and viable explanation based upon the dangerousness model can be derived from the research evidence as was

Table 23: **Numbers Receiving Sentences of Varying Severity Following Interracial and Intraracial Rape**

Racial Composition of Rapist and Victim	Most Severe Sentence	Intermediate Sentence	Least Severe Sentence
Sample 1			
Black-on-white	17	9	3
Black-on-black	9	12	12
White-on-white	11	6	16
Sample 2			
Black-on-white	15	23	15
Black-on-black	6	19	23
White-on-white	6	16	19

Note: Severity of sentence was determined independently for each sample by breaking down the distribution of sentences as evenly as possible into three categories. Sample 1: most severe = life, intermediate = 20-35 years, least severe = less than 20 years. Sample 2: most severe = greater than 20 years to life, intermediate = 20 years, least severe = less than 20 years.

the case with sentencing for black criminals who murder white victims.

For a beginning, examination of sample 2 cases revealed that severity of sentencing for black criminals who raped white women corresponded to their average level of dangerousness: severe sentence = 3064.93, intermediate sentence = 2613.74, least severe sentence = 2045.07. These widely variant index scores ($p<.001$) draw attention to behavior associated with dangerousness as the basis for frequent severe sentences received by the black interracial rapist rather than judicial bias. A closer look at the relationship between severity of punishment and dangerousness of men who rape women of the same race revealed no comparable effect. Combining over both intraracial groups because of similar sentencing patterns, men who raped women of their own race and received severe sentences (M=2573.42), intermediate sentences (M=2545.24), and least-severe sentences (M=2309.88) were much alike in index-defined dangerousness. The correspondence between sentencing severity and dangerousness of the criminal is restricted to black interracial rape. I will turn now to the question of whether criminal circumstances can be identified for this racial pattern that will corroborate the role of dangerousness and explain more severe punishment.

Dangerousness scores of the interracial and intraracial rapists in the second sample, along with ratings of physical and psychological brutality of the sexual aggression (0-8 scale) and the amount of resistance offered by the female victim (0-4 scale), were based upon information drawn from randomly-selected files of prison inmates. The average scores for these three parameters of crime are found in Table 24. Statistical analysis of the tabled data revealed much the same result for each characteristic. There was a progressive increase in dangerousness of the criminal, brutality of the act, and victim resistance as you consider the white rapist targeting a white victim, through the black intraracial rapist, to a high in each case for the black sex-offender who rapes a white woman. This variation was significant ($p<.05$) for the brutality and resistance variables and approached reliability for dangerousness ($p<.10$). Comparison at the extremes between black and white men who rape white victims proved significant at the 5% level or less for all three characteristics. These results portray differences in criminal/victim racial patterns that identify black sex-offenders who rape white women as more dangerous, more brutal in their crimes, and as confronted with greater resistance from their victims.

The latent issue of bias against blacks in the Georgia courtrooms

Table 24: Dangerousness of the Rapist, Brutality of the Act, and Resistance of the Victim for Cases of Interracial and Intraracial Rape

Criminal and Crime Characteristics	Interracial Rape (Black Rapist - White Victim) (N=53)	Intraracial Rape (Black Rapist - Black Victim) (N=48)	Intraracial Rape (White Rapist - White Victim) (N=41)
Dangerousness	2630.83	2512.85	2317.34
Brutality of act	5.57	4.79	4.15
Resistance of Victim	2.34	2.04	1.51

for crimes of rape is at least cast as open to serious doubt. The black rapist who targets a white woman seems to merit the more severe punishment he receives because of his more malicious treatment of his victim. There is one more finding, however, that warrants consideration in attempting to tease apart dangerous conduct and sentencing bias in an effort to understand the serious punishment accorded to black interracial rapists.

Closer examination of the convictions imposed on the three categories of rapists revealed that the sex-offenders often forced their victims to submit to acts of sodomy (oral and anal sex) in addition to raping them, presumably involving vaginal penetration; in such cases, the men were convicted on independent charges of rape and sodomy. Twenty-one of 53 (40%) black rapists were convicted on both counts when their victims were white, 13 of 41 (32%) white men both raped and sodomized their white victims, and 7 of 48 (10%) of the black sex-offenders who targeted black women engaged in both sex crimes.

Consideration of the sentences given to the sex criminals in our sample revealed that the courts took the combination of a rape and sodomy conviction seriously, but they seemingly did so rather selectively for black men who aggress sexually against a white woman. Again, the specter of courtroom bias is encountered. To illustrate this using the trichotomized punishment categories that appear on Table 23, sentences given to black men who forced their white victims to engage in acts of rape and sodomy qualified as "most severe" (more than 20 years in prison) in 57% (12 of 21) of the cases. Black-on-white sex crimes in which sodomy was seemingly not involved resulted in "most severe" court verdicts only 9% (3 of 32) of the time. Rapists who victimized women of their own race elicited a similar pattern of verdicts from the courts. Considered together, black and white sex-offenders who exposed their same-race victims to multiple sex acts received "most severe" sentences 17% (4 of 23) of the time. Intraracial sex-offenders found guilty of rape alone were punished severely in a similar 12% (8 of 67) of the cases. The 57% figure for "most severe" sentences given both a rape and sodomy conviction for a black sex-offender with a white victim does raise the possibility of prejudicial sentencing when compared to the 9-17% figures for the other intraracial sex-offender groups guilty of multiple sex-offenses.

It seems clear that black sex-offenders who have demeaned their white victims by forcing them to submit not only to rape but also to sodomy are far more likely to be severely punished than intraracial rapists who have done the same thing. Dangerousness proved to be a viable alternative to prejudicial sentencing in this analysis as well. Black men who both raped and sodomized their white victims were exceedingly dangerous according to the model ($\underline{M}$ = 2934.38, $\underline{N}$ = 21); black rapists who did not subject their white victims to sodomy were far less dangerous ($\underline{M}$ = 2431.62, $\underline{N}$ = 32, $\underline{p}$<.001).

Examination of intraracial rape cases revealed that men whose sex-offenses included both rape and sodomy were actually less dangerous ($\underline{M}$ = 2103.20, $\underline{N}$ = 20) than men convicted of rape alone ($\underline{M}$ = 2515.42, $\underline{N}$ = 69, $\underline{p}$<.01). Obviously, it is not written in stone that subjecting women to a more debasing range of sexual demands is necessarily linked to criminal dangerousness of the sex-offender. When black men rape and sodomize white women, dangerousness definitely seems to be a factor ($\underline{M}$ = 2934.38); when either black or white men do the same to a woman of their own race, dangerousness is an unlikely factor ($\underline{M}$ = 2103.20).

The assumption that sexual aggression involving both rape and sodomy is more harmful to the victim than rape alone need not depend upon a more-is-worse interpretation of sexual aggression by a male investigator. The brutality represented in the rapist's treatment of the victim offers a more objective way of establishing whether the coercion of rape and sodomy involves more vicious treatment of the victim than rape alone, particularly in black-on-white sex-offenses. Sex crimes involving both rape and sodomy showed these average brutality scores on a 0-8 scale: black-on-white crimes = 5.81, black-on-black crimes = 4.95 and white-on-white crimes = 4.42. Crimes of rape alone resulted in these average brutality figures: black-on-white crimes = 5.41, black-on-black crimes = 4.70, and white-on-white crimes = 3.86. Overall analyses revealed an effect for nature of the sexual aggression ($\underline{p}$<.05). Women who were raped and sodomized were more brutally victimized whatever the racial pattern of sex-offender and victim. However, the average brutality rating for black sex-offenders with white victims reaches an absolute value (5.81) that implies special malice for these very dangerous men. The more serious punishment they receive seems justified in light of the more extensive violation of their victims and the more brutal manner in which they consummate their crimes.

Overview

The various data sets that were explored in this chapter allow for arguments either way as far as the importance of race is concerned in understanding dangerousness in my theoretical model. It was found in one type of analysis, for one criminal characteristic and crime attribute after another, that the white-versus-black distinction was unimportant in understanding the relationships with dangerousness. Whatever effects emerged when the white criminal received our attention were duplicated for black criminals. The only distinction between the races was the elevated dangerousness scores of black criminals which consistently exceeded those of white offenders. The systematically higher dangerousness scores of black criminals in our research samples may or may not turn out to be of importance in understanding the risk of harm to the victims of crime. Conclusions regarding racial differences in behavioral potential must be rendered very cautiously unless one wishes to stir debate that goes well beyond the scientific arena.

The second approach to deliberating the issues of race in modeling criminal dangerousness involved consideration of criminal/victim racial patterns for crimes of murder and rape. When the analysis is extended to include the race of both the criminal and the victim, there seems little doubt that race enters into the way that dangerousness relates to crime and punishment for these serious violent offenses. Dangerousness was prominently noted in the black offender but was a defining feature of their within-crime level of violence only when the victim was white. The seemingly excessive punishment handed out to black murderers whose victims are white or black rapists who target white women may stir accusations of judicial bias in some quarters, but dangerousness of the criminal looms as an alternative in both cases.

That black offenders who target white victims are more dangerous by index score is basic to the argument of alternative explanation, but other information garnered from the criminal circumstances corroborates this relation between racial pattern and dangerousness. Black men who kill white victims and are given the death penalty end up doing this in a brutal way even if the victim shows little resistance; these are the most dangerous men based upon the model. Black men who rape white women and do so in an especially malicious way by cruelty and the further debasement of sodomy are the most dangerous of sex-offenders. There seems to be good reason to expect criminally-dangerous black men, by definition both highly antisocial and limited in their cognitive capabilities, to be especially menacing to whites. Cruelty to the more helpless white murder victims and more brutal and humiliating treatment of women subjected to sexual aggression point to that conclusion. The highly dangerous black criminal seems to carry an enmity toward whites that mobilizes an especially aggressive brand of violence.

Perhaps it would be fitting to end this chapter bearing on issues of race and dangerousness by noting that the evidence has taken me full-circle as far as the considered role of social prejudice is concerned. The assumption of judicial prejudice against blacks, in light of the disproportionate punishment when violence was directed toward whites, was challenged by dangerousness findings. It was suggested in fact that the evidence on racial patterns in violent crime might signal a prejudice against whites and add to the motivation of very dangerous black criminals. Animosity toward the white race fueled by a history of collective discrimination, individualized experience, and political exaggeration may prove compelling to someone who is lacking in restraint both because he is antisocial and cognitively limited. A hostility toward the victim may join forces with a deterioration in the criminal transaction to make a bad situation worse for the white victim confronted by an ultradangerous black offender.

Chapter 9

Dangerousness and Gender

The program of research into a multifactorial model of dangerousness reported thus far in this book has focused exclusively upon the male criminal. There are good reasons for this exclusive focus; primary among them is that males commit a majority of the crimes in our country despite being a minority of the population. Understanding male criminality in general and violence in particular therefore qualifies as a more important goal from the point-of-view of eventual deterrence, since men represent a more compelling concern. The logistics of scientific data collection also placed a priority on accessibility of subjects. Parole assessment made an important contribution to my research program, and this source of data rarely included women prisoners.

After I finally completed a few studies bearing upon female crime and its treatment within the criminal justice system, I came to recognize the importance of at least examining the dangerousness model as it may apply to women. Theoretical explanation of female dangerousness promised to be different, perhaps more complicated, than was found to be true for men for two very good reasons. Physical aggression has traditionally been underrepresented in female behavior, and the way that this would influence the relationship between dangerousness and criminal violence remained to be seen. Besides this complication, cultural changes in the woman's role in western societies over the past 20-30 years included some modification of gender-based behavioral differences. Expression of physical aggression might be subject to change as a distinguishing gender characteristic. The question remained whether changes in the criminal behavior of women (or the way these changes are perceived) would increase or decrease the common relevance of the dangerousness model to both men and women.

I shall set the stage for presenting the studies concerning dangerousness and criminality in females by considering two earlier investigations of women, crime, and punishment. This review may help you to understand why the dangerousness model might have more ready application to males and confront a sterner challenge with females.

Preliminary Studies of Female Criminality and the Response of the Criminal Justice System

Study of criminal impulsivity, type of crime, and punishment by gender. My first examination of female criminality and its treatment within the Georgia criminal justice system (Heilbrun, 1982) compared 618 women criminals with 678 males. The sample included those who had committed offenses between 1963 and 1978 for women and between 1955 and 1976 for men. The female cases were drawn randomly from the files of women gaining parole during two two-year periods -- 1972-1973 and 1977-1978. Those achieving parole at the earlier time had committed their crimes, been convicted, and received sentences before the women's movement became a major force in our country between 1970 and 1973. I intended to control for the possible effects of the women's movement on criminal behavior and courtroom decision by including the 1977-1978 parole cases, since crime and sentencing in these cases tended to follow the arrival of feminism in the early 1970s. Looking back at this study, I am able to see that I unduly limited its implications by simply trying to balance the possible effects of the women's movement by combining the pre-post groups. I ignored the possibility of examining these effects directly by comparing pre-feminism and post-feminism crime and punishment for women. This oversight was remedied years later (Heilbrun & Gottfried, 1988; Heilbrun & Heilbrun, 1986) in studies that will be described on pages ahead.

The male criminals that served as the basis of comparison for the women offenders had been drawn from the same files, but they represented an aggregate of smaller independent samples of men collected for a number of previously published studies of parole outcome (Heilbrun, 1978; Heilbrun & Heilbrun, 1976; Heilbrun, Heilbrun, & Heilbrun, 1978; Heilbrun, Knopf, & Bruner, 1976). The timing of their criminal acts and courtroom verdicts was such as to guarantee substantial numbers of male criminals from the period before the early 1970s as well as following the surge of feminism, matching the female sample.

The research interest in this 1982 study focused upon the treatment of women within the criminal justice system, a topic that gained priority in the 1970s because of gender issues arising from the women's movement. Adler (1975) observed differences in the treatment of women at the time of arrest, in the courtroom, and following incarceration. Females were thought to be overrepresented among status offenders (Chesney-Lind, 1977) and to receive lengthier sentences because of overprotectiveness within the judicial system (Armstrong, 1977). Adler herself reached the opposite conclusion when she observed the more lenient treatment of women because of a chivalrous attitude adopted by the courts. Smart (1977) also detected a more lenient and protective approach to women offenders taken by the criminal justice system. An overprotective response to the female criminal had been generally observed, then; whether overprotection led to more severe or more lenient treatment was apparently a matter of where researchers directed their attention.

My interest in the 1982 study was in testing an assumption of impulsivity that had been introduced to explain why women criminals should be treated differently than men within the criminal justice system (Pollak, 1950; Smart, 1977). Women were believed to be generally more impulsive than men, and this poorer inhibition of impulses was expected to show itself by spur-of-the-moment criminality. Since offenses based upon lapses in self-control are dealt with more leniently by the courts than premeditated crimes (e.g., manslaughter versus murder), it followed that women should receive less severe punishment than men. In other words, women should be protected from their own impulsivity.

There was a complication in this explanation of more lenient sentencing for female criminals that argued for specifying the type of crime being considered. When the impulsiveness of various types of crime is quantified by examining the actual circumstances surrounding their occurrence, it becomes clear just how widely they vary as far as being spontaneous or planned even for men who are supposed to be more self-controlled (Heilbrun, 1979). One of the more obvious contrasts is the greater impulsivity of violent crimes relative to more premeditated nonviolent offenses. If women are generally more impulsive in their criminal behavior than men, as some were contending, we are left with the question of whether this holds equally true for more impulsive violent acts as well as more premeditated property crimes?

The methodology of this 1982 study comparing crime and punishment across genders was devised in such a way as to address three questions relating to female criminality. First, is female criminality generally more impulsive than the criminal behavior of men for all crimes as was commonly assumed? Second, if not for all crimes, is greater female impulsivity as likely to show up in violent as in nonviolent crimes when they are compared to men? Third, are women extended more lenient punishment than men following conviction for the same crime, and does this depend upon whether the crime is one committed more impulsively by women?

Ratings of the impulsive or premeditated nature of female and male crime were based upon 4-point scales. A trained rater assigned a probability to each crime following review of the criminal circumstances in the offender's file. The ratings could range from "clearly not planned and clearly a spontaneous act" (score = 1) to "clearly planned and clearly not a spontaneous act" (score = 4). Point 2 indicated an act that was probably spontaneous, whereas point 3 was reserved for an act that was probably premeditated. These ratings proved to be quite reliable as gauged by a correlation between raters (r = .94). The punishment analysis considered the actual amount of time that the criminals remained under crime-related restraint, including prison and subsequent parole, before being released. Race did not influence the findings, so black and white criminals were combined in the female and male groups.

Table 25 offers crime-by-crime comparisons of women and men as far as impulsiveness/premeditation ratings are concerned as well as the cumulative time spent in prison and on parole following conviction. The impulsive or premeditated character of female crime, using male criminal norms as standards, was not in line with preexisting assumption that held female criminality to be the result of a deficit in self-control. The validity of this assumption depended upon the kind of crime being considered. Violent crimes involving physical aggression (murder, manslaughter, assault) were more impulsive when committed by a woman (all ps < .01). Criminal violence involving only the threat of physical aggression (robbery) and the three nonviolent crimes (burglary/theft, forgery, drugs) were associated with the opposite effect. Female criminals were more planful in their

Table 25: Degree of Impulsivity/Premeditation of Major Crimes and Subsequent Punishment for Males and Females

| Crime | Impulsivity-Premeditation[a] | | | Time in Prison and on Parole[b] | | | |
| | Females | | Male Norms[c] | Females | | Males | |
	N	M		N	M	N	M
Murder	6	1.50	2.51	12	9.44	63	13.55
Manslaughter	72	1.67	2.32	124	3.77	50	4.98
Assault	32	1.95	2.56	60	2.01	74	4.16
Robbery	35	3.44	3.16	39	2.70	100	5.57
Burglary/Theft	77	3.56	3.26	136	1.47	271	2.98
Forgery	69	3.91	3.36	131	1.69	40	2.69
Drug	60	3.90	3.25	116	1.60	61	1.62

[a] On a 4-point scale from clearly impulsive to clearly premeditated

[b] Time from initial incarceration to release from parole given in years

[c] Based upon a total of 275 felons

criminal activities than their male counterparts ($\underline{ps}$ < .05-.001).

The evidence suggests, then, that women are not criminal simply because their impulsiveness makes them generally vulnerable to antisocial acts. Only crimes of physically-aggressive violence involve greater female impulsivity relative to men. Otherwise, the results showed female criminality to be more premeditated. The violence findings are especially striking, since the male norms on Table 25 reveal the greater impulsivity of crimes involving physical aggression for men. Spontaneity of female violence was demonstrated even when compared with these diminished standards of restraint. Of course, it was equally striking that women departed from stereotype with respect to nonviolent criminality despite the generally premeditated nature of property crimes. Female criminals not only failed to fit the impulsive stereotype, but they were more planful than men; this was true despite the premeditated character of male property crimes.

Examination of the punishment data does confirm a general leniency accorded women in their punishment during the period covered by this study. For every crime save drug offenses, the woman served less time in prison and on parole than did the man (all $\underline{ps}$ < .01). Although other gender-related factors besides the stereotype of female impulsiveness could play a role in punishment, this set of findings does seem in line with the observations of chivalry toward women in our criminal justice system of the 1970s or before. Given the half-truth involved in assuming that impulsivity of women sets them apart from men in their criminal conduct and merited punishment, the general leniency shown to women by the criminal justice system was misplaced. Females who committed crimes of aggressive violence tended to do so on impulse, according to this 1982 evidence, and should have been punished less than males who are more inclined to plan such crimes. However, this gender difference in criminal conduct is reversed in nonviolent crimes and even in the case of violence without physical aggression (robbery). Given that fact, women should have been treated with greater severity than men within the system, at least to the extent that premeditation plays a role in how crimes are punished.

Study of punishment by gender for violent and nonviolent crimes before and after the women's movement. The Heilbrun (1982) study that was discussed in the previous section took the women's movement into consideration as a potential influence in the treatment of the female in America's criminal justice system. It did so by controlling for the timing of the crime and conviction through combining both pre-feminism and post-feminism cases in the same sample. The premise underlying this methodological decision was that pressure for equal treatment of women and men as far as social rights are concerned may be accompanied by parallel pressure for equal responsibility in conforming to the law rather than chivalry and overprotection. Whatever the merit of this premise, it was not directly tested in the 1982 study. The results revealed a pervasive and continuing leniency to the punishment accorded the female criminal without respect to a pivotal point in our social history.

In order to cast light upon whether the changing role for women did influence their treatment in the criminal courts, a follow-up study (Heilbrun & Heilbrun, 1986) was conducted in which the time factor became an independent variable available for analysis rather than a control variable dictating sampling procedure. In essence, the second study allowed us to consider whether the leniency toward women found previously for all crimes except drug offenses -- whether it resulted from original sentencing or from subsequent decisions concerning time to be spent in prison or on parole -- did or did not change with the impact of feminism in the early 1970s. Of equal importance, we were concerned about whether the changes, if observed, followed the dictates of jurisprudence that stipulate less punishment for a given crime if the act is impulsive rather than preconceived. This calibration effect would be demonstrated if women receive more lenient sentences for a violent crime involving physical aggression where they are more impulsive than men. At the same time, women should not be spared punishment when convicted of other crimes in which they are more premeditated in their actions then men. In short, the follow-up study considered whether feminism as a social movement brought more egalitarian treatment of men and women by the criminal justice system in which punishment depended upon the nature of the crime rather than a pervasive leniency toward woman.

The records of 4813 criminals who had served their sentences in Georgia Prisons were drawn; this number included 1450 violent males and 177 violent females along with 2877 nonviolent men and 309 nonviolent women. Three violent crimes were represented; two involved physical aggression toward the victim (manslaughter, assault), and the third involved the threat of physical aggression (robbery). Murder was excluded from consideration because of the infrequency of this sentence for women in our sample. Nonviolent crimes included burglary/theft, forgery, and drug offenses. The 1970-1973 span of years again was adopted as the critical transitional period for the women's movement, but "early period" (pre-movement) and "late period" (post-movement) definitions took on somewhat different meanings for the two categories of crime.

Time-sampling procedures for contrasting length of incarceration for men and women convicted of violent crimes required more extended periods because of longer prison terms. The early period for violent offenses required that crime/conviction/imprisonment were completed during the 1960s. All decisions relating to punishment were completed before the women's movement began to assume central importance. The late period for violence meant that crime, sentencing, and incarceration all were a matter of record after 1970. Comparison of prison terms for nonviolent criminals involved an early period from 1970-1973 and a late period from 1974-1978. Thus, the comparisons of both violent and nonviolent criminals of both sexes were made between nonoverlapping groups, as far as the timing of crime and punishment is concerned, with differing recognition of the 1970-1973 transition period as the dividing point.

Table 26 presents the average time in prison spent by women and men convicted of major crimes during two time periods -- before or while feminism was becoming a national focus and later when there had been greater time for equal-treatment by gender to have permeated the criminal justice system. For the most part, the figures in this table affirm a growing appreciation of criminal impulsivity or premeditation in punishing both men and women after the women's movement attracted national attention. Violent crimes of manslaughter and assault, in which women act more impulsively than men, resulted in shorter prison terms ($ps < .001$) before and after the women's movement. This gender difference in punishment should not have changed, and it did not. Nonviolent crimes, found to involve even greater planning for women than men in the earlier study, showed a shift in punishment that better reflected this criminal dynamic. Eventually, women at least received equal punishment for all three types of nonviolent crime.

The one exception to the generally improved calibration of punishment for female criminals in the post-feminist years was found in the treatment accorded to women convicted of robbery. It was found earlier that women not only matched the premeditation of male robbers but actually were more planful in this kind of violent crime that involves only the risk of physical aggression. Yet the woman received

Table 26: Time in Prison[a] Following Conviction for Various Crimes by Men and Women as a Function of the Women's Movement

Crime	Early Period				Late Period			
	Males		Females		Males		Females	
	N	M	N	M	N	M	N	M
Violent Crimes								
Manslaughter	101	46.71	34	24.72	237	47.03	60	25.94
Assault	91	34.02	17	12.71	120	32.63	28	21.04
Robbery	224	57.81	12	25.00	677	43.57	26	30.65
Nonviolent Crimes								
Burglary/Theft	271	25.28	56	10.29	1898	22.11	57	19.68
Forgery	40	24.00	54	13.33	145	18.68	41	17.32
Drugs	61	13.97	46	12.04	462	18.83	55	19.38

[a] In months

less severe punishment in the 1982 study, and she was still incarcerated for shorter periods in this 1986 follow-up ($p<.001$). Even so, there may be a trend here. The nearly 33-month difference in prison time for men and women convicted of robbery in the early period dwindled to about 13 months in the post-feminism group. Male robbers were averaging over 14 months less time in prison for their crimes in the post-feminist period, but incarceration of women increased by almost six months for this crime. All in all, the criminal justice system made vast progress in eliminating gender bias in their punishment.

Female Criminality and the Dangerousness Model

I have not lost sight of why I considered these earlier studies of female criminality and its punishment as a prologue to discussing gender issues relating to the dangerousness model. Their special relevance resides in the finding that female violence involving physical aggression is far more likely to represent an impulsive act than is true for men and that this continues to be recognized by the criminal justice system in terms of less severe punishment. That this gender difference was empirically documented is especially noteworthy, since violent crimes tend to be impulsive for men to begin with when compared with nonviolent offenses.

The ultra-impulsive character of physical violence in women can be understood in terms of female socialization, because conventional role expectations deter physical aggression. The woman who adopts conventional standards would find it difficult to calculate engaging in physical violence; more likely, violent action would occur on impulse and be driven by emotions of the moment. At least, several researchers who examined female criminals, especially violent ones (Adler, 1975; Hoffman-Bustamente, 1973; Simon, 1975; Weis, 1978), have found a rejection of feminine role expectations. The erosion of traditional sex-role commitment in women, encouraged by feminist influence, could help explain more dangerous behavior in contemporary women, since conventional constraints upon physical aggression would be expected to decrease. Campbell (1986) documents the increased prevalence of physical aggression in British girls and young women for example, well beyond what would have been expected in the pre-feminist years. It was somewhere in the ebb and flow of changes in expressing physical violence that I might have anticipated a problem of fit for the dangerousness model and contemporary female criminals.

Actually, the studies concerning post-feminism expressions of physical violence hold somewhat ambiguous implications for the dangerousness model. At a very general level, it is uncertain in what way the change in social expectations for women might be expected to influence the applicability of the model to females. Would less constraint upon aggression make women criminals more like men in the premeditation of violence and allow the dangerousness model to be more readily extended to both genders? Alternatively, would this relaxed constraint upon aggression simply add to the already impulsive character of female violence, further distinguish between women and men, and somehow complicate the construct of dangerousness as applied to violent criminality in women? A direct look at female dangerousness and the impact of the women's movement was called for.

Dangerousness in women and criminal violence. Heilbrun and Gottfried (1988) made an initial effort to examine the applicability of the dangerousness model to female criminality. A problem arose because for reasons not yet clear to me only about 20% of the female criminals sampled in the study had an IQ in their file, an omission encountered only rarely with men. This fact, discovered after the data collection had been completed, made it impossible to use the standard multiplicative dangerousness index with reliable numbers of women. The published 1988 paper was restricted to considering antisociality alone and is only marginally relevant to the model. At this point, I shall present two approaches to the Heilbrun and Gottfried data that did not appear in the journal article but prove informative enough to include in the present discussion. A more definitive body of evidence that will not require apology will be reported later.

The files of 217 Georgia women prisoners were drawn randomly from two sources -- those who had committed crimes between 1965-1971 before feminism attained national prominence and those whose crimes occurred in 1980-1985, long after the women's movement crested in the early 1970s. The early sample averaged about 30 years of age, 9 years of education, and was made up of 61 black and 49 white women. The late sample of women also averaged around 30 years of age, had a mean education of about 10 years, and presented a racial composition of 62 blacks to 45 whites. Type of crime (violent versus nonviolent) was introduced into this study as an independent variable. We originally wanted to determine whether violent women would emerge as more dangerous than nonviolent women, as had been the case for male criminals, and whether this difference would be found for women criminals before and after the pivotal years for the women's movement.

One possibility left to me for examining the relationship between criminal violence and dangerousness in women by post hoc analysis of the Heilbrun and Gottfried data is to concentrate on the 42 subjects that had IQs in their records. This number was made possible by ignoring the period of time during which the crime was committed. Scoring dangerousness by antisociality scores based upon file information and IQ, violent women (N=20) presented an average dangerousness score of 2785.55, substantially higher than the 2302.32 average of the nonviolent females (N=22). Violent women were more dangerous than nonviolent women (p<.05), conforming to the dangerousness model and to results obtained using male criminals.

The second option for post-hoc analysis of the Heilbrun and Gottfried data having relevance to the dangerousness model is to substitute educational attainment for IQ. This allows me to introduce the early-late distinction in commission of the crime into the analysis of female dangerousness for the entire sample. Education is a far from perfect indication of tested intelligence quotient which has served me so well in quantifying dangerousness. This may be especially the case in a sample of criminals whose antisocial conduct and lagging motivation could have influenced the time they spent in school without regard to how bright they were. Nevertheless, there was a significant correlation (p<.01) between IQ and years of formal schooling (r=.42) for the 42 women who had been tested for intelligence. You can gain a more graphic impression of what this moderate correlation means if the relationship is examined in another way. On average, women who completed high school showed an IQ of 106, an 80 IQ if they failed to go beyond the 8th grade, and an intermediate IQ of 95 given in-between schooling of 9-11 grades. Even though the correlation between IQ and grades completed was not high, rather clearcut differences in average intelligence were disclosed across levels of schooling.

Dangerousness scores in the overall analysis represented the product of antisociality and years of education after both raw scores were converted to standard scores with a mean of 50 (SD=10). A small number of the original subjects had to be eliminated from this analysis, because their educational levels were indeterminate from the record.

Table 27 includes the dangerousness scores of female felons convicted of violent and nonviolent offenses committed before and after

Table 27: Dangerousness of Violent and Nonviolent Female Criminals Before (1965-1971) and After (1980-1985) the Prominence of Feminism

Crime	Early Period		Late Period	
	N	M	N	M
Violent Crimes	38	3074.63	53	2615.32
Nonviolent Crimes	60	2367.83	49	2455.98

NOTE. - Dangerousness scores based upon antisociality ratings and years of formal education (as a substitute for IQ) the transition into feminism in 1970-1973. Statistical examination of the mean dangerousness scores divulged two things. Overall, violent female criminals were more dangerous than their nonviolent peers (p<.001). The results of the analysis using IQ scores for part of the sample were confirmed with the full sample when education was substituted for intelligence in the dangerousness index. Women who commit more harmful aggressive crimes, like men, proved to be more dangerous than women guilty of nonviolent offenses.

Further analysis of the Table 27 scores disclosed an interaction between type of crime and time period (p<.05) that complicates interpretation of the overall dangerousness effect. The striking disparity in dangerousness of violent women relative to property offenders before the surge of feminism (p<.001) was no longer evident by the 1980s. Instead, only a modest elevation of index scores was found for violent women. This interaction would suggest that modified social role expectations after the early 1970s diminished the applicability of the dangerousness model to women. However, the changes indicated by the data seem to be restricted to the dangerousness of women committing violent crimes as their average index scores dropped over 450 points in the late period. The dangerousness of women with nonviolent offenses remained much the same over time and social change. It might be noted that the drift in model applicability occurred for black and white women alike; seeming effects of the women's movement were the same for both races.

At this point I will review the complicating factors in applying the dangerousness model to women suggested by the three studies discussed thus far in this chapter. I regret being repetitious, but I want to be sure that the reader is prepared for the fourth study that lies ahead. In that study an improved methodology allowed us to uncover some rather curious evidence regarding female criminality and dangerousness in contemporary America. As it turned out, the dangerousness model did not lack relevance to the female criminal. In one way the fit was even better than was true for males. It was only when murder as the most violent of crimes received our attention that the dangerousness model seemed to falter for women.

The first complicating factor verified by our research was the greater impulsivity of female violence when it is compared to that displayed by men, especially significant because male violence itself tends to be generally impulsive compared to nonviolent offenses. This gender difference holds true for violent crimes involving actual physical aggression (murder, manslaughter, assault, battery) but not for robbery in which physical violence is potential rather than actual. Female involvement in robbery actually tends to be more premeditated. The problem of applying the dangerousness model to women criminals introduced by extreme impulsivity would be the greater likelihood that physical violence will erupt simply because of a momentary lack of constraint, probably fostered by heightened emotions. A momentary lapse in cognitive function might suffice as an explanation of physical violence for the woman without invoking antisociality and more enduring cognitive limitations, the theoretical mainstays of criminal dangerousness. Although the dangerousness model includes limited self-control as a cognitive factor in male violence, this factor may detract from prediction within a generally impulsive female population.

The seeming decline of model applicability to female violence after the early 1970s could be the result of loosened constraints upon female physical aggression brought about by the women's movement, as many have suggested. This adds a second complication. As some women reject their traditional social role, they relinquish a deterrent to violence implicit in the more passive, nurturant, and relationship-oriented qualities of femininity. The predictability of violence from the dangerousness model might be expected to deteriorate as women become more attuned to engaging in physical aggression and violent crime. Violence would less and less be reserved for the woman flawed in values and cognitive functioning as emotion-driven impulsivity and more permissive attitudes toward physical aggression combine. Whether emergent female violence would have the same dynamics as for the male criminal remained to be seen.

The third complication in fitting the dangerousness model to women comes from the more lenient treatment of violent women in the criminal courts. As I have emphasized, the more impulsive character of aggressive violent crimes committed by women may go a long way in explaining the differential sentencing between women and men. To the extent that leniency from the courts following violent crime has become an expectation as well as a fact, the deterrent value legal punishment has for the woman, whatever it might be, must suffer. Deterrence of female violence may have been compromised even further in America over the past 20 years, since our data will show that the most serious crimes of physical aggression are frequently directed toward men who have abused the female perpetrator. If the courts consider an abused history to be a mitigating factor in conviction or sentencing for a violent crime and this becomes a matter of popular awareness, these counteraggressive acts by women could be even less deterred by anticipated punishment. It might also be argued that the attention given to male abuse of women and to the woman's right to resolve this damaging arrangement has encouraged counteraggression in females who are not otherwise dangerous.

A more critical test of the dangerousness model for women. Heilbrun and Kors drew a new sample of female criminals in 1991, taking advantage of what was learned from earlier research in the program. The sample included 116 women who had been sent to prison after 1981. Despite some methodological blemishes, we had found evidence that the dangerousness model was applicable to women before the revision of social values in the early 1970s, at least as far as discriminating between violent and nonviolent criminals. In this new study interest was focused upon the curtailed explanation of female violence after that transitional period. Accordingly, we chose to examine violent criminality in women that was clearly embedded within a post-feminist American society.

The methodology in this study allowed for several types of analyses that had proven fruitful in considering male dangerousness as well as others that seemed especially relevant to post-feminist violence for women. The relative dangerousness of female criminals who had committed violent crimes at varying levels of severity was examined, a discrimination that had been used to validate the model in the case of males. The prediction of parole outcome also drew our attention, again falling back on a line of evidence that fulfilled theoretical expectations for men. Contemporary issues in female violence were addressed by considering criminal and victim characteristics along with the circumstances of aggressive crimes.

The female criminal cases were drawn from Parole Board files at three levels of violence severity as defined by parole guidelines. The three violent crime categories were similar to those constituted for males yet not identical, because contact sexual offenses frequently committed by men (rape, sodomy, incest, child molestation) are rarely encountered among female criminal convictions. This required some rearrangement of specific crimes in the severity categories for the women, although they remained nonoverlapping as far as rated severity was concerned. Severe violence was defined by a conviction for murder as with men (N=40). Intermediate severity included violent crimes of aggravated assault or battery, voluntary manslaughter, cruelty to children, kidnapping, and armed robbery/robbery by intimidation (N=40). Low-severity violence˙ was represented by two crimes -- involuntary manslaughter and vehicular homicide, neither involving intent to kill (N=36). The three crime categories included matching numbers of black and white criminals. Preliminary analysis revealed no significant effect of race in the female results, so black and white women were considered together within the violence groups with a single exception. Race of the criminal did emerge as significant at one point and was introduced as an independent variable.

In addition to considering the nature of criminal offense, the data search was attentive to victim characteristics for each of the violent acts whenever this information was recorded in the file. Victim gender was of special interest along with age, since we eventually wanted to examine two victim groups -- adult males and others (women and children). We also sought evidence of prior abuse of the female criminal by her male victim. This information regarding victim and criminal circumstance was used to test the conjecture that contemporary female violence toward men might not follow the dictates of the dangerousness model because of the number of these crimes that are more instigated by prior abuse than personality-based dangerousness.

Let us first consider the evidence regarding the relative dangerousness of female criminals who have committed violent offenses of a less or more serious nature. Dangerousness scores, based upon IQ and antisociality ratings taken from the women's files, did reveal significant variation (p<.05) among the severity groups. However, average scores for the three categories did not correspond to theoretical expectations or to the previous findings for violent male criminals. Women who murdered had an intermediate dangerousness mean (2416.25); those demonstrating mid-severity violence (assault, voluntary manslaughter, robbery, and kidnapping) were the most dangerous (2637.82); and women guilty of unintentional violence (involuntary manslaughter and vehicular homicide) presented a low index score (2193.28). It is the failure of the high-severity violence group of murderers to assume a paramount position in the progression of dangerousness scores that is at odds with theory regarding the risk of harm to a victim and with the evidence for men. Without considering women who had murdered their victims, the discrimination findings would have been consistent with both the dangerousness model and earlier male results. Intermediate-level aggression was associated with higher dangerousness in the woman than low-severity violence (p<.01).

These erratic results for women confirmed my concern regarding model applicability to female violent criminality in post-feminist America. Supplementary analyses involving victim and criminal characteristics, as well as circumstances of the crime, took on special significance in understanding the relationships between dangerousness and contemporary female violence. In my mind it seemed necessary to take cognizance of women's attitudes toward men in the 1980s in order to make better sense of the data. I would explain this conviction by the following observations.

The emphasis upon gender equality has encouraged a shift in attitude, largely negative in character, as men have been held responsible for the social problems faced by women. Hostility toward men, deserved or not, is readily apparent. This social phenomenon of hostility and accountability is exemplified by the increasing unacceptability of physical, sexual, or psychological abuse of women by the male, often in the context of a continuing domestic or work relationship. Increasing intolerance of male abuse would be expected to activate counteraggressive motives in which a need for self-protection or revenge leads the abused woman to act in a violent way toward her tormenter. To the extent that female aggression can be understood as a response to abuse by a male, the dangerousness model is unnecessary to explain that source of violence.

These thoughts regarding female violence in the 1980s led to two analyses that promised to cast light upon the violence-severity findings. The first of these considered whether the index score was less consistent with degree of harm involved in women's violent crimes when men were the victims. Three sets of violent female criminals were compared on the index score. One set had directed their aggression toward a man, and for a second set the victim was another female or a child. Only crimes for which the gender and age of the victim would be evident to the criminal were considered. The nature of violence ran the gamut from murder, voluntary manslaughter, assault/battery, and robbery down to involuntary manslaughter. For added information, a third set of violent women were included in the analysis -- those who were convicted of vehicular homicide. In these cases, the characteristics of the victim(s) are likely to be unknown, and violent intent is not involved.

Women who behaved violently toward other women or children were by far the most dangerous among the groups categorized according to victim characteristics (M=2764.52, N=27). Those who targeted men as their violence victims were less dangerous according to model specifications ($\underline{M}$=2410.38, $\underline{N}$=78). Crimes of vehicular homicide in which victim characteristics would play no part were committed by remarkably nondangerous women ($\underline{M}$=1561.82, $\underline{N}$=11). The overall analysis revealed significant ($\underline{p}$<.001) overall variation among the three sets of criminals; of greater importance, there was a reliable difference in dangerousness between females who were criminally violent toward women and children and those who targeted men for violence ($\underline{p}$<.05). The vehicular-homicide criminals departed radically from both of these groups on the index score ($\underline{p}$s<.001). The dangerousness model, then, seems viable when applied to violent female criminals except when men are the victims. Unfortunately for the model, most of the victims of female violence (74%), when victim characteristics were known to the women, turned out to be men.

The second type of analysis bearing upon specifics of the violent crime and limitations of the model focused exclusively upon women who had been convicted of murder. You may recall that it was this specific group that fell out of line with the theoretical expectations of the dangerousness model, since the women who inflicted maximum harm upon the victim did not display the highest level of dangerousness. The present analysis considered whether the failure of the model may have resulted in part from the presence in this group of women who had suffered abuse from their male victims and who might be compelled by that experience to kill their abuser. Dangerousness would not be as relevant to the dynamics of extreme violence in women if that were true. As it turned out, men were the victims in 27 of the 40 murders, and in 13 of these cases evidence of prior abuse by the male was found in the record. The average dangerousness score for women who murdered their male abuser was 2057.62. The 14 women who killed men without any reported provocation by prior abuse averaged 2617.07 on the index, and the difference was significant ($\underline{p}$<.05). It certainly appears that a history of abuse by a man limits the power of the dangerousness model in explaining the behavior of female murderers in post-feminist America.

Having found evidence that a history of abuse may compromise the applicability of the dangerousness model to women who murder their male abusers, the question remains whether the same abuse factor might be more generally responsible for the unsystematic variation in index scores among violence severity levels for women. Accordingly, all violent females, no matter what their crimes might have been, were eliminated from the second analysis of dangerousness by severity level if a history of abuse by the male victim was verified. It was at this point that a race effect became evident requiring black and white females to be analyzed separately. Table 28 reports the average dangerousness scores by race for female criminals at three levels of violence severity with cases involving prior abuse by the male victim dropped from consideration. This left cases in which the victims of violence were women, children, and nonabusing men.

These tabled data reveal a compelling and systematic relationship between how much harm is extended to the victims of female violence and the dangerousness of the woman ($p<.001$) once male abusers are eliminated from consideration but only for white women. The counterpart analysis for black violent women did not produce the same level of significance ($p<.05$), and the mean dangerousness scores across severity levels failed to correspond to theoretical prediction. Black women committing intermediate violence were more dangerous than low-severity black women ($p<.05$), but murder continued to defy model-based expectations.

The prediction of parole outcome from dangerousness scores represented the second approach to model validation that was investigated for women. In contrast to the discrimination analysis, parole outcome offered uncomplicated support for the dangerousness model. There were 98 women who had been released on parole during the period covered by our sampling. Three types of outcome were distinguished, representing distinct qualitative differences in adjustment to parole. Success was defined by an accommodation to requirements that earned the woman a discharge from parole ($N=50$). Failure represented a return to prison following parole revocation for technical violation or criminal recidivism ($N=23$). An intermediate group of women were continuing on parole at the time the sample was drawn for this study ($N=25$). These women had neither qualified for discharge by that time nor had their paroles been revoked.

The dangerousness mean scores for the three parole-outcome groups are found in Table 29 along with a breakdown of these results by race of the woman on parole. Race was maintained as an independent variable here only to insure that the sometimes effect found when considering violence severity was not operative in parole outcome. The prospective relationship between dangerousness and parole risk was a convincing one as far as validating the dangerousness model was concerned. Those who failed on parole were the most

Table 28: Dangerousness of White and Black Female Criminals at Three Levels of Violence Severity After Dropping Cases Having Male Abusers As Victims

Levels of Violence Severity	White Female Criminals		Black Female Criminals	
	N	M	N	M
High[a]	11	2746.55	15	2671.60
Intermediate[b]	17	2292.65	17	2970.35
Low[c]	16	1763.94	12	2582.75

[a] Murder
[b] Aggravated assault or battery, voluntary manslaughter, kidnapping, cruelty to children
[c] Involuntary manslaughter, vehicular homicide

Table 29: Dangerousness in Female Criminals and Adjustment to Parole

Adjustment to Parole	All Women Combined		White Women Only		Black Women Only	
	N	M	N	M	N	M
Success	50	2113.50	34	1973.62	16	2410.75
Neither Success nor Failure	25	2577.76	8	2557.25	17	2587.41
Failure	23	3138.91	6	2924.50	17	3214.59

dangerous followed by women of intermediate parole status; successful parole outcome was associated with the lowest index scores. The differences in dangerousness were highly significant (p<.001), widely variant, and systematic according to theory whether all female criminals were considered together or separately by race.

There are two conclusions that I believe to be warranted from the 1991 Heilbrun and Kors data regarding criminal dangerousness in women. For one, there is ample evidence to suggest that the dangerousness model has applicability to the female as well as the male. The validating prediction of parole outcome for women based upon their index scores was convincing and matched the same finding for men. Discrimination by model specifications for severity of violence was less impressive for the woman than for her male counterpart unless complications in female violent criminality within contemporary America are considered. However, allowance for cultural revision since the early 1970s went a long way in bringing the criminal violence of women under the explanatory umbrella of the dangerousness model.

The second conclusion bears upon the number of special factors that emerged as relevant to explaining contemporary violence of women in terms of dangerousness. In general terms, the theoretical model worked best when the victims of female aggressive crimes did not include men who had previously abused the criminal. Restricting all victims of violence to other women, children, and nonabusing men brought discrimination into theoretical alignment with the dangerousness model for all the women studied. Even murder, particularly vexing upon initial analysis, fell in line with the model given this refinement, at least for the white murderers.

The explanation for these added complications in model application to female violence seems simple enough. Tolerance for men and their abusive behavior has dropped to a lower ebb since the women's movement arrived, and the potential for male-directed counterviolence in the female seems to cut across a more diverse set of women as far as their psychological makeup is concerned. It seems that many women, who are not dangerous by model specification, may act violently out of anger, fear, or resentment directed toward men, often instigated by abuse. However, if victims of violence other than men, especially abusing men, are considered, victims are not so closely tied to female role revision. In such cases the aggressive criminal behavior of women corresponds more closely to the dictates of the model. Taking these complications into consideration works better in explaining contemporary violent crime in terms of dangerousness for the white female criminal than was true for her black counterpart.

The conclusion that the female findings simply contribute to a more complex model of dangerousness for women than for men that requires added consideration of victim characteristics along with different race issues may understate the case. We should not forget that impulsivity adds yet another complication setting female violent criminality apart from male violence, although the difference is a matter of degree and not kind. Even though I have no empirical evidence to bring to bear, I certainly would expect the extreme impulsivity of female violence to interact with these victim characteristics to promote an even more involved explanation of dangerousness as a precursor to violence in the exceptional case of an abusing male victim. Men who abuse women arouse the level of emotion that would trigger impulsive violence; these women otherwise offer small risk of physical aggression.

Chapter 10

Dangerousness and Mental Disorder

The issue of whether mental disorder influences the risk of dangerous criminal behavior is often dismissed in one way or another, either by compassion on the one hand or by stereotype on the other. Although the question posed is an important one, it has not attracted as much definitive research as it deserves. One still confronts pockets of denial from those who assume responsibility for the plight of mentally-disordered individuals and contend that this type of disability is unrelated to dangerousness. The contention that a mentally-disordered person is no more likely to harm others than the person without psychiatric problems is an understandable view for those who are interested in maintaining sympathetic attitudes toward the mentally ill. Compassion would suffer if crime and violence were seen as defining properties. On the other hand, stereotypes of madness abound which sustain concern about the dangers posed by the mentally disordered. Although many would consider the terrifying violence of a deranged stalker in "slasher" movies to be unrepresentative, who among them would elect to build their homes next to a mental hospital?

Statistics are rarely cited in the debate concerning mental disorder and whether it is unrelated or related to physical aggression. Even if they are, they are very likely going to be more convenient than critical. In order to bring compelling data to bear regarding the dangerousness of the mentally ill, it would be necessary to include a number of observations that are rarely reported. The obvious place to start -- the number of crimes, particularly violent ones, that are committed by someone with a diagnosed mental disorder -- is only the beginning. Going beyond this, how much violence occurs in mental institutions or special prison units where such behavior is not treated as a criminal violation but rather as a symptom of disorder? Alternatively, how much criminal violence in the community is committed by individuals suffering from undiagnosed mental disorders, and how much violence in general prison populations could be traced to undiagnosed conditions? The point that I am trying to make here is not that mental disorder includes an inherent risk of dangerous behavior or that it does not. I am only proposing that the issue is open to investigation and should not be settled by compassion or negative stereotype.

The possible importance of mental disorder to the understanding of dangerous behavior is actually implicit in the theoretical model that has been explored in this book. As I have reiterated more often than the reader may have found necessary, the model proposes that a host of ineffective cognitive traits are basic to the understanding of criminal dangerousness as they combine their effects with antisociality. These cognitive functions, not as yet fully articulated or confirmed individually, have been represented by IQ as a shorthand marker. The basic assumptions here are simple and defensible. People with lower tested intelligence will be generally less capable in their cognitive functions; these functions, thought of as the "higher mental processes," subserve behaviors that contribute to effective social adaptation. Planning, anticipation of behavior, implementation of alternative strategies, social transactional skills including social judgment, and self-control are but a few of the cognitively-mediated acts that have been proposed as important to effective behavior, criminal or otherwise.

The use of an available IQ as a marker of cognitive effectiveness was adopted, because individual cognitive assessment was beyond my logistical resources in the first place and was not among the options made available to me in the second place. However, cognitive limitations can result from many things other than poor intellectual endowment. Cognitive impairment can be a temporary disability associated with strong emotional states or a more permanent disability caused by insults to the cerebral cortex. In between these extremes of permanency, mental disorder may include the compromise of cognitive skills and styles either as part of the primary symptomatology or as a secondary effect of the person's disorder or efforts to compensate for the disorder. In other words, mental disorders may introduce a greater risk for criminality, according to the model, because they add to the kind of cognitive limitations that can make people dangerous. Although I will not emphasize the point, mental disorder of more serious proportions could contribute to more dangerous criminal conduct by influencing the value system as well. People with delusions of persecution might be expected to revise their values regarding attainment through merit and fair play as an example.

The expectation of cognitive aberrations in people suffering from mental disorders should not be taken as a blanket warning regarding criminal dangerousness, however. The rest of the formula for dangerousness within the model should be kept in mind. The special risk of criminal dangerousness in general and violence in particular would only be anticipated theoretically if the mentally-disordered person were also antisocial. The debate over the role of mental disorder in dangerous criminal behavior, to whatever extent it goes beyond anecdote, usually focuses entirely upon the kind of psychological changes that are symptomatic of one or another disorder. Little attention is likely to be paid to premorbid or current level of antisociality.

Without some clarification from research evidence, I do not believe that we can anticipate whether mental disorder makes any special contribution to criminal dangerousness as it is defined by the model. Considered as a whole, the mentally ill could be no more dangerous than others in the general population as their advocates claim or might even gravitate toward either extreme of dangerousness. It all depends upon the unknowns of cognitive impairment and antisociality that have received comment and the way that they interact.

Two types of investigations bearing upon the relationship between mental disorder and dangerousness within a forensic population will be described. The first will involve a comparison between the dangerousness of two types of violent offenders. Men who had committed a violent act but were subsequently found not guilty by reason of insanity (NGRI) will be compared to men who also committed violent crimes but were found guilty, held responsible for their actions, and sent to prison. The question here is whether the dangerous conduct of mentally-ill men does follow from impairment by their disorder, as the courtroom decision suggests, or can it be associated with high criminal dangerousness? The second set of studies will consider a number of psychometric indicators of aberrant thinking within samples of prisoners as they may vary with levels of dangerousness. This type of analysis will approach the issue of how dangerousness and mental disorder relate from the opposite direction; are more dangerous prisoners more aberrant in their mental functioning?

Dangerousness of Men Convicted for Violent Offenses and Men Not Held Responsible for Violence by NGRI Verdicts

The criminal court system provides an opportunity to examine the dangerousness of men judged to have suffered from a mental disorder at the time they engaged in violent behavior and not held responsible for their otherwise criminal conduct. The verdict of not guilty by reason of insanity presumes that the violence had its origins in the psychological abnormalities of the individual that rendered him incapable of forming intent or exerting control over his impulses. Without being capable of reasonable intent or control, the person cannot perform a legally criminal act. Investigation of the assumptions underlying the NGRI verdict (Heilbrun, M.R., 1986; Heilbrun & Heilbrun, 1989) focused upon the dangerousness of violent men who received this form of acquittal.

My present purposes are not served by emphasizing the controversial aspects of the NGRI verdict as was the case for the earlier papers. The data from this study are well-suited to the consideration of dangerousness and violence in the mentally disordered, however. The original investigation by Mark Heilbrun compared two groups of men who had been confirmed as violent by the criminal courts. One group was diagnosed as mentally ill at the time of their violent act and the other was not. The straightforward question to be answered for present purposes is whether men who were mentally-ill at the time they committed a violent act differ in level of dangerousness from men who engage in violence without evidence of disorder?

Three possible answers could be found, and each would bring its own brand of conclusions concerning mental disorder, dangerousness, and the potential for violence. NGRI patients who have engaged in violence could be less dangerous than violent felons. That would suggest that mental illness itself promotes violence, as the courtroom verdict would have us believe, and provide evidence for exception to the dangerousness model as an explanation for victim harm. NGRI patients and violent criminals could look much the same on the dangerousness index; that finding might indicate that the NGRI acquitees and the criminals in prison tended to engage in violence for much the same reason and that mental disorder had little to do with it. Those who argue that the mentally ill are no different from the general population as far as violent proclivities are concerned could take heart from such findings. Finally, NGRI patients could prove to be more dangerous than men convicted of violent crimes. That result would encourage us to recast the issue in new terms in which dangerousness plays an even more compelling role in violence of the mentally ill. Greater dangerousness in NGRI patients would seem to reduce concern about the risk of violence from mental disorder per se, since another source of risk has been identified. However, this would be illusory, because the coalescence of extreme dangerousness and mental disorder would remain as a source of concern.

Samples. The data bearing upon the issue of dangerousness and mental illness as sources of violent conduct were collected from two samples of men under the jurisdiction of the criminal justice system. One was made up of 55 forensic patients at three mental hospitals in Georgia and Florida. This sample included men who had committed a violent act which had inflicted or threatened physical harm to a victim but for whom an NGRI verdict had been rendered. Psychological assessment of these patients had been completed by hospital staff between 1981 and 1985. The prisoner sample was comprised of 204 men assessed for parole between 1973 and 1985. They had been convicted of violent crimes involving the same aggressive acts as committed by the NGRI patients.

The two samples were similar in average age (33 and 35 years) and mean education (patient sample = 11 years, prisoner sample = 10 years). However, a control for level of education was introduced into the major analysis, since this demographic variable was found to be sufficiently correlated with the dangerousness index score (r = -.46, $p<.01$) over the combined samples that the discrepancy could have influenced the results. Age showed no correlation with dangerousness. The racial proportions for the samples varied substantially. More violent blacks had received NGRI verdicts than violent whites, whereas a higher proportion of whites than blacks appeared in the prisoner sample. However, there was no relationship between race and dangerousness in this particular study, so the disproportionality was ignored.

The dangerousness index. The instruments used with the NGRI patients had been chosen by staffs of the three participating hospitals to satisfy their own assessment goals, and testing data were made available through their generosity. Three hospital sources were required in order to accrue a sufficient number of men who had received an NGRI verdict for a violent act and for whom the psychometric batteries allowed us to approximate the dangerousness index. All patients had taken the Minnesota Multiphasic Personality Inventory (MMPI) so that the Psychopathic Deviate scale could be standardly employed as an antisociality estimate. The Socialization scale from the California Psychological Inventory was not available for use as a complementary score within the subtractive antisociality measure. NGRI patients also had completed an IQ test, usually the Wechsler Adult Intelligence Scale (Wechsler, 1955).

Incompetent interpersonal transaction, a variable that has received substantial theoretical attention within the model and had added to the prediction of dangerous prison and parole conduct (Heilbrun & Heilbrun, 1985), was gauged from the Social Introversion (Si) scale of the MMPI. Given the required departures from standard dangerousness scoring, it was decided that the variable could best be quantified by an index that included all three scores, hoping to bolster its strength. IQ, Pd, and Si score arrays were transformed to standard score distributions with a mean of 50 ($\underline{SD}$=10) based upon the total patient/prisoner sample. The revised additive index, Pd + Si + IQ, was devised so that higher scores indicated greater dangerousness; this involved inverse transformation of the IQ score so that lower IQs brought higher standard scores.

A preliminary check on the equivalence of the revised dangerousness index to scores derived by standard procedures was possible. Prison conduct records for the 204 violent criminals in our study were determined by examining their accumulation of formal disciplinary reports. Each report was scored for this analysis along a misconduct scale ranging from nonconfrontational violation of prison rules (score = 1) at the low end to levels of violent engagement (scores = 6 or 7) at the high end. The cumulative scores were then split into thirds, defining those who were low ($\underline{N}$=68), intermediate ($\underline{N}$=65), and high ($\underline{N}$=71) in dangerous prison conduct. The means for the revised index scores provided by these three groups -- $\underline{M}$=143.40, $\underline{M}$=148.60, and $\underline{M}$=157.28 -- fell in the theoretically anticipated order and varied significantly ($\underline{p}$<.01). This replicated our earlier findings using the multiplicative index based upon the product of Pd minus So and Culture Fair IQ standard scores. Substitution was encouraged, since it was possible to demonstrate the same predicted relationship using the standard and the revised dangerousness index.

Dangerousness of the violent NGRI patient. The central question being addressed in this analysis is whether men who have engaged in criminal violence but have not been held responsible for their acts because of mental illness are distinguishable from ordinary violent criminals as far as dangerousness is concerned. Table 30 includes the dangerousness scores for the violent NGRI patients and violent prisoners, each group broken down into educational levels by the total sample median. (This levels analysis controls for the significant relationship between years in school and dangerousness reported earlier.) Statistical comparison revealed that the NGRI patients were higher on the index than prisoners ($p<.001$), and this proved to be the case at both educational levels. Violence in men judged to be mentally disordered when they acted was associated with even greater dangerousness than the criminal violence of men who were sent to prison for their crimes.

The conclusion drawn from the comparison of NGRI patients and prison inmates at the time the original papers appeared in the 1980s held that given the heightened dangerousness of the mentally-ill men, their violence was better explained by this psychological risk factor than by their mental condition. Adjudicating their violence by holding them unresponsible when, considered overall, the NGRI men would have been even more criminally dangerous than their presumably sane counterparts in prison, represented an enigma for the criminal justice system.

The conclusion from these results that I have come to favor in preparing this book is that the NGRI sample included men whose violence was overdetermined. Not only were these patients extremely dangerous in keeping with the model of dangerousness, but they also were more likely to be further impaired in their cognitive functions (and social values) as part of their disorders. The combination of cognitive limitations signalled by diminished intelligence and by diagnosed mental disorder could produce a broader array of cognitive deficits relevant to violent criminal transaction; alternatively, this collaboration could result in more profound impairment of a few critical cognitive skills. In either case, the sample of NGRI men would represent an even more dangerous group according to theory than their higher dangerousness scores suggest. This conclusion does not absolve the NGRI verdict; that verdict still blurs the responsibility for violent conduct by considering only mental disorder and not criminal dangerousness.

What the evidence has shown is that there are some very risky men who suffer from mental illness. I would go beyond that to conclude that mental disorder may provoke special risk for violence but

Table 30: Dangerousness of Violent Patients Receiving the NGRI Verdict Compared to Violent Criminals

Group	High Education (11 Grades or More)		Low Education (10 Grades or less)	
	$\underline{N}$	$\underline{M}$	$\underline{N}$	$\underline{M}$
NGRI Patients	36	161.25	19	163.58
Prisoners	81	143.86	123	153.85

only when its effects are superimposed upon dangerousness as specified by the model. This conclusion should not be taken to mean that mental illness generally does nor does not hold much of an inherent risk of harm to others. It does mean that if there is concern about risk in a mental patient, it becomes especially important to establish level of dangerousness.

The kinds of research that would allow a clearcut examination of the combined risk presented by model-defined dangerousness and mental illness are not available to me. A well-controlled baserate study of violence within a mentally-ill population to see whether high dangerousness is associated with excessive violence relative to a population of ordinary violent criminals would be a start. This kind of study could clarify the prevalence of violent crimes as well as the degree of harm inflicted upon the victims when the mentally-ill criminal is also highly dangerous. Individual assessment that considered an array of cognitive skills and styles would also prove interesting in order to test the idea that low IQ in the mentally disordered leads to more extensive or profound cognitive limitations that might translate into dangerous criminality. Such evidence being unavailable to me, what I shall do is explore the relationship between index-defined dangerousness and abnormal cognition in a criminal population. In this approach we will take a look at specific forms of cognitive deviance in ordinary criminals at the extremes of dangerousness associated with NGRI violence.

Considering the relationships in a prisoner population between levels of dangerousness and individual cognitive abnormalities that might foster violence could accomplish two things. First, it could serve as a replication of sorts for the finding that the mentally ill who engage in violent behavior are extremely dangerous according to the model. Now we will examine the reverse proposition; violent criminals who are extremely dangerous will be abnormal in their thinking. A second advantage to be gained from the reverse mode of analysis is an increased specification of what is meant by abnormal in terms of thought processes and quantification to show how deviant the extremely-dangerous criminal might be. In the NGRI investigation, psychological abnormality remained nonspecific except as implied by verdict and subsequent patient status in a mental hospital.

Dangerousness and Psychometric Indicators of Cognitive Abnormality

The MMPI and CPI protocols from individual prisoners that provided the Pd and So scale scores defining antisociality in many of our studies also included a great deal of other psychometric information. Some of this information had a bearing upon strengths and weaknesses of cognitive functioning and offered a very different look at the relationship between disordered behavior and dangerousness as defined by the model. Research questions that were to be answered in the first set of analyses concerned whether a difference in the quality of thought would be found if criminals with violent and nonviolent criminal histories were divided by levels of dangerousness and compared.

I will then turn to a series of inquiries that will build upon the initial findings regarding abnormal thought and criminal dangerousness. Independent evidence from a new sample of sex-offenders was drawn in order to replicate and extend the initial psychometric findings. Next, the implications of these analyses of dangerousness and abnormality were pursued by considering the demographic characteristics of a subset of sex-offenders identified as both high in dangerousness and aberrant in thought, the prototype for excessive risk. Finally, I will return to the data from the NGRI study to consider whether disturbed thinking, measured psychometrically, may work in concert with dangerousness to promote prison misconduct in violent criminals.

Dangerousness and psychometric correlates of disturbed and effective thought. A sample of 174 sets of personality tests were drawn from accumulated protocols in my parole assessment files and were analyzed with the valuable assistance of Allison Foster and Jill Golden who were working in my laboratory at that time. The sampling of MMPIs and CPIs was random except for the requirement that half had to have committed violent crimes; 87 violent and 87 nonviolent male prisoners were included. Dangerousness scores were determined by the standard procedure in which Pd-So scores and IQ scores were multiplied after transformation. These index scores, in turn, were assigned to three groups with a third of the subjects in each group. The cutting score for high dangerousness fell at 2761, scores between 2100 and 2760 designated prisoners as intermediate in dangerousness, and a score of 2099 or less defined low dangerousness. Having a tripartite split insured that the highest group would include only men who were extremely dangerous. A further breakdown within each level of dangerousness by race was introduced when preliminary analysis revealed that the results differed slightly across black and white racial lines. Numbers in the resulting six subgroups will be found on the forthcoming table.

The psychometric indicators of disturbed thinking were taken from the MMPI and included four scales that have been termed the "psychotic tetrad" (Dahlstrom & Welsh, 1960). These involve four of the original scales that were developed as measures of psychotic disorder involving aberrant thought processes. The four scales include Paranoia (Pa), Psychasthenia (Pt), Schizophrenia (Sc), and Hypomania (Ma), and the types of disturbed thought reflected in their scores can be described as delusional, obsessive, bizarre, and flighty. The tetrad score is given by the sum of the four scale scores. The dysfunctional thinking associated with an elevated psychotic tetrad score would almost inevitably prove disruptive in the planning or execution of a criminal activity.

Effective thinking was inferred from two scales appearing on the CPI. Intellectual efficiency (Ie) gauges the extent to which the individual makes use of the intellectual potential available to him. Psychological-mindedness, on the other hand, reflects the degree to which the individual considers and understands the dynamic meaning of manifest behavior, his own or that of others. It was assumed that more efficient use of intellectual resources and a more reflective approach to understanding behavior represent examples of positive cognitive functioning. These scale scores were added to measure effective thinking; lower scores would represent impaired cognition.

Table 31 presents the psychotic tetrad and effective-thinking scores for the sample of criminals split into three levels of dangerousness scores and black/white racial groupings. An overall dangerousness effect was revealed ($p<.05$) for the tetrad score with more dangerous criminals providing clearer indications of disturbed thinking. This effect appeared for both racial groups, although there were different types of curvilinearity within each group. The white prisoners who were most dangerous (upper third) also were singularly high in their tetrad scores. For black prisoners, the elevated tetrad scores appeared for men who were at the upper and intermediate thirds of the dangerousness dimension. The conclusion remains the same in either case, however; more dangerous prisoners according to the model qualified as more disturbed in their thinking.

The effective-thinking scores reported in Table 31 also conformed to expectation. A significant dangerousness effect ($p<.001$) reflected the low intellectual efficiency and poor psychological-mindedness of

Table 31: Dangerousness and Scores on the Psychotic Tetrad and an Index of Effective Thought for White and Black Criminals

Indices of Thought	High Dangerousness				Intermediate Dangerousness				Low Dangerousness			
	White		Black		White		Black		White		Black	
	N	M	N	M	N	M	N	M	N	M	N	M
Psychotic Tetrad[a]	36	240.61	22	231.68	39	217.54	18	235.89	46	215.15	13	222.23
Effective Thinking[b]	36	92.44	22	88.50	39	98.31	18	88.66	46	107.52	13	98.85

[a] Sum of scores on Pa, Pt, Sc, and Ma scales of the MMPI
[b] Sum of scores on the Ie and Py scales of the CPI

the most dangerous prisoners which gave way to increased effectiveness for the least dangerous. This relationship appears in linear form for the white criminals and is curvilinear for black criminals but, again, a general conclusion is warranted. The dangerous criminal is lacking in effective thought qualities relative to less dangerous criminals.

The two scales chosen to represent positive thought qualities for this analysis have a special relevance to the assumptions of the dangerousness model. Dangerous offenders have been presented as lacking the intellectual resources to avoid criminal circumstances in which violence would be a serious risk or to extricate themselves from such circumstances without escalating this risk. According to our psychometric data, even the deficiencies in intelligence implicit in the lower IQs of dangerous criminals do not fully describe their limitations. Lower intellectual efficiency scores suggest that they do not utilize even these limited resources very well.

Psychological-mindedness represents a tendency to consider the meaning of behavior at some level more profound than surface appearance, first-impression, and stereotype. Finding limited psychological-mindedness at the extreme of dangerousness is reminiscent of earlier evidence that the most dangerous of criminals lacked empathic skills (Heilbrun, 1982). Empathy has to do with an understanding of another person's feelings through shared (vicarious) experience and offers a guide to effective social transaction. Now we are informed that the dangerous criminal not only lacks empathic skills that would contribute to social awareness through vicarious experience but also falls short in analyzing his social observations. The dangerous criminal seems to bring very little basis for compassion or anticipation of victim behavior into the criminal transaction.

Dangerousness of male sex-offenders, age of their female victims, and disturbed and effective thought. A second psychometric probe of the relationships between quality of thought and criminal dangerousness was conducted, encouraged in part by the wish to replicate the findings of the first study. In order to go beyond sheer replication of previous findings, the MMPIs and CPIs were drawn for a different type of criminal and other psychometric indicators of impaired thought were added to the analysis.

The MMPIs and CPIs of male sex-offenders were selected for this probe. The contact sex-offenders were further subdivided into those who aggressively victimized adult women (rape, sodomy, or related sex crimes) or female children (child molestation, incest, or related sex crimes). Thus, gender of the victim was held constant, but victim age was left to vary. While I know of no strong case to be made for the greater role of cognitive impairment in sex-offenders who target other adults or those who seek out children, I found it possible to argue either way before looking at the data.

It might be argued that committing sex crimes against children is likely to involve more deviant cognition, because something as objectionable as adult sexual involvement with a child represents a more radical departure from norms of social conduct. The child molester and incestuous adult violate any number of mores concerning appropriate sexual objects, protection of children in general, and the special obligations of parenthood in particular. The more inappropriate the behavior, the more disturbed the mentation that underlies it. This by no means is meant to depict rapists as epitomizing sound mental processes by process of elimination. However, their sexual targets, adult women, are at least in the mainstream of normal preference based upon age and nonfamilial status. It is in violating the woman's rights and in the force and brutality of the act that the rapist flaunts social convention and law.

On the other hand, our own data has demonstrated child molesters and perpetrators of incest, considered overall, to be less dangerous than rapists. Less dangerousness, in turn, has been associated with sounder mental functioning relative to more dangerous criminals. Arguably, this might suggest that sex-offenders who rape are more likely to show aberrant cognitive qualities.

This debate calls for examination of the relationship between dangerousness and thought abnormalities within each sex-offender group. By isolating highly dangerous sex-offenders of each type, any special contingencies between dangerousness and aberrant thought for either group should come to light. Previous comparisons that found rapists to be more dangerous than child-molesters were based on total groups. This would lead us to expect fewer highly-dangerous men among those who molest children, but the question remains whether the highly-dangerous child molesters that are found will present a more or less perilous level of dysfunctional cognition relative to dangerous rapists.

The psychotic tetrad ($\underline{Pa}$ + $\underline{Pt}$ + $\underline{Sc}$ + $\underline{Ma}$), taken from the MMPI and the indicator of effective thinking ($\underline{Ie}$ + $\underline{Py}$), combining two scale scores from the CPI, were considered as before. In addition, a third metric of deviant thinking, based upon a different rationale, was added.

This index included the $\underline{F}$ scale score from the MMPI and the Communality scale (Cm) from the CPI. These scores convey the extent that the responder selects options on keyed items that are unusual relative to the general population. The higher the $\underline{F}$ score and the lower the Cm score, the more unusual the choices made by the individual. Since the two scales are scored in opposite directions to indicate deviant choice, a subtractive index ($\underline{F}$ - Cm) was devised. Higher (plus) scores are most readily interpreted as reflecting peculiar thought with extremely high scores suggesting a weird quality to the person's thinking.

Alternative interpretations of high scores on the $\underline{F}$-Cm index are possible. For example, a high number of unusual responses to the questionnaires could result from a test-taker's choice of responses without regard to what the items say. This could follow from a number of invalidating circumstances such as an inability to read, carelessness, or even choosing to respond randomly. None of these is a likely explanation for systematic elevation in $\underline{F}$-Cm scores across subjects in this sample. In the parole assessment procedures reading ability was carefully checked before the personality tests were administered. Either careless or random responding was counteracted by continuous monitoring of the prisoner's test behavior during which time anything other than serious commitment to the test would likely be noted. Finally, disregard for testing instructions, mirrored in carelessness or random selection, would be extremely unlikely in parole assessment; prisoners take their release options seriously.

The 61 sex-offenders who had raped or sodomized women victims ("rapists") and 58 sex-offenders guilty of molestation or incest who had victimized female children ("child molesters") were trichotomized, using the combined distribution of dangerousness scores. Dangerousness levels were defined by the following scores: high dangerousness (>2744), intermediate dangerousness (2144-2744), and low dangerousness (<2144). The number of men in each of these groups and average scores on the three indices of abnormal or effective thought are presented in Table 32.

Statistical testing first addressed the issue of replication. The finding that highly dangerous criminals were more aberrant in their cognitive functions, established previously with a sample of assorted violent and nonviolent male offenders, was again apparent in a sex-offender sample. Sex-offenders, whether they victimized female adults or children, revealed the same relationship as before between

Table 32. Dangerousness and Cognitive Impairment in Sex-offending Men Who Victimize Women and Girls

Level of Danger-ousness	Sex-offenders Who Victimize Women						Sex-offenders Who Victimize Girls					
	Psychotic Thought[a]		Effective Thought[b]		Deviant[c] Thought		Psychotic Thought		Effective Thought		Deviant Thought	
	N	M	N	M	N	M	N	M	N	M	N	M
High	24	234.62	24	89.08	24	7.58	16	253.94	16	85.50	16	24.94
Inter-mediate	20	225.75	20	98.20	20	.75	19	228.16	19	94.32	19	-1.53
Low	17	215.41	17	102.82	17	-1.82	23	227.09	23	106.56	23	-3.17

a (Pa+Pt+Sc+Ma) from the MMPI
b (Ie+Py) from the CPI
c (F-Cm) from the MMPI and CPI, respectively

dangerousness and abnormal thought. Those who were more dangerous displayed higher scores on the psychotic tetrad ($p<.01$), lower scores on scales depicting effective thought ($p<.001$), and higher scores on an index measuring deviant thought ($p<.001$). The relationship between abnormal psychiatric status and extremely high dangerousness scores established in the NGRI study has now been confirmed and replicated in psychometric studies of criminals in prison that found extremely high dangerousness to be related to thought abnormalities.

Despite the fact that the two sex-offender groups looked much alike in the way that disturbed thinking increased with dangerousness, Table 32 does provide one distinguishing feature. The most dangerous tier of child molesters displayed a singular degree of cognitive impairment when compared with less dangerous molesters. Perhaps even more compelling, the average impairment scores for the most dangerous molesters were substantially higher than the averages for highly dangerous rapists, significantly so for two out of the three indices. Dangerous child molesters presented much higher scores on the psychotic tetrad (253.94 versus 234.62, $p<.001$) and the index of deviant thinking (24.94 versus 7.58, $p<.001$), the two scores most readily understood as markers of aberrant cognition. The effective-thinking index comparison revealed somewhat more diminished scores for highly dangerous child molesters (85.50 versus 89.08), although the difference proved unreliable.

Despite the fact that child molesters, considered collectively, present less risk of harm to their victims than rapists according to the dangerousness model, the present results encourage special caution regarding heterosexual molesters who prove exceptions and do qualify as highly dangerous. These child molesters by present analysis are singularly aberrant in their thought processes. The collaboration of dangerousness and disturbed thinking introduces special concern for the victims of their sexual crimes. Abnormality of thought would be expected to add to the risk already inherent in the excessive dangerousness of this tier of molesters as both contribute to impairment. It is discomforting to contemplate a situation so onesidedly under the control of an offender as an adult male molesting a female child that involves such a mentally-flawed criminal.

Homosexual child molesters had not been included in the comparison of sex-offenders on psychometric indices of aberrant thought, because there were so few available test protocols for men who sexually abused boys. However, the rather striking results of examining heterosexual molesters by dangerousness levels sent me back to the basic pool of sex-offenders in order to see whether this effect could be duplicated in whatever number of homosexual child molesters were available.   Since only 15 homosexual offenders were in the parole assessment file, I split this group only into two rather than three levels of dangerousness.   The median split for this analysis fell at a rather low 2352, using the raw score to standard score conversion tables for the larger sample of sex-offenders that had just been analyzed. More highly dangerous homosexual child molesters ($\underline{N}$=7) and their less dangerous counterparts obtained the following respective average scores: psychotic tetrad -- 244.71 and 230.25; effective thinking -- 76.86 and 110.62; deviant thinking -- 25.14 and -7.00.   Although the tetrad difference was not statistically significant, both of the remaining differences were ($\underline{p}$<.01).   These disparities were obtained despite the lack of extremely high dangerousness in the upper tier and the small numbers.   These comparisons along with those reported previously support the same conclusion.   Although men who molest children are generally not dangerous according to model specifications, those who are also show up as especially abnormal in their thought processes. This convergence of deviant sexual preferences, dangerousness, and aberrant thought is apparent whether the child molesters target girls or boys.

   Follow-up examination of risk for the highly-dangerous heterosexual child molester.   The evidence for uniquely aberrant thinking in more dangerous child molesters brought me as close as possible within my psychometric analyses of men housed in Georgia prisons to a subset of criminals that might compare with NGRI patients. Child molesters who showed a level of dangerousness comparable to the NGRI sample also presented psychometric evidence of highly deviant cognitive functions.   The psychometric scores were so elevated in fact as to make some form of mental illness a real possibility for the 16 heterosexual child molesters in the upper tier of dangerousness. These scores for the few homosexual molesters who were more dangerous in a relative if not an absolute sense looked every bit as foreboding.   These observations encouraged a follow-up analysis that was not feasible with the NGRI patients in which information would be examined relevant to criminal risk and taken from earlier dangerousness studies.

   A new sample, including highly dangerous heterosexual child molesters, and a low-dangerousness comparison group of heterosexual molesters, was drawn in order to further establish whether this subset of violent criminals was as great a risk to society in general and their victims in particular as the combination of dangerousness and thought abnormality conveys. Molesters of female children from the Hollmann-Wasieleski samples were assigned to two extremes of dangerousness using the same cutting scores as for the high dangerous (>2744) and low dangerous (<2144) tiers in prior Table 32. Child molesters who obtained middle-range dangerousness scores were not included in the analysis.

Four variables relevant to criminal risk were considered. The research question in each case was whether 47 high-dangerous and 42 low-dangerous molesters of female children could be distinguished in a way predictable from the dangerousness model. Socio-economic status of the criminal is important theoretically, because it reflects a decreased emphasis on mainstream prosocial values in underclass America relative to the middle-class. Lower-class priorities are also less likely to involve reinforcement of cognitive functions involved in planning, self-control, and skillful social transaction. Given these class differences, the dangerous child molester with a lower-class affiliation would find himself in a social context that is more tolerant of the antisociality intrinsic to dangerousness as well as the cognitive deficits implied by lower IQ and aberrant thinking. Lower-class membership could be seen as contributing to the flawed value/cognition systems in the first place and to sustaining their imperfections as time passes.

The state system for classifying criminals according to social-economic class assigned lower-class status to the most-dangerous molesters in 87% of the cases with only 13% having middle-class origins. The least-dangerous molesters had lower-class backgrounds 57% of the time and middle-class in 43% of the cases. The difference in proportions was reliable (p<.01) and paired extreme dangerousness in child molesters with probable lower-class membership. The antisociality and cognitive limitations implicit in a high dangerousness score and otherwise deviant thought processes are more likely to be sustained, even nourished, by lower-class experience.

Intoxication during commission of the sex crime was examined next. Intoxication of the criminal should increase risk for the victim to the extent effective cognition is diminished. In a molester who already represents a risk to children in keeping with the dangerousness model and is further compromised cognitively by signs of mental illness, inebriation could prove to be the last straw. Impairment of cognition could become so great and prosocial values so completely disregarded that risk to the child becomes menacing.

The percentage of men who showed any degree of alcohol or drug intoxication when they molested their girl victims was ascertained for men at both extremes of dangerousness. Highly-dangerous molesters were intoxicated 63% of the time; low-dangerous men were reported to be intoxicated in 38% of the cases. These figures distinguish the two groups ($p<.05$) and suggest that dangerous child molesters commonly suffer from three sources of impairment when they confront young girls. They display the enduring cognitive limitations and antisociality that enter into criminal dangerousness, show the aberrant thinking that verges on mental illness and that may further distort values, and often enhance these limitations by acting while intoxicated. Assuming these sources of impairment work in unison, the value system and higher mental processes that are supposed to govern human social conduct may be a shambles in the highly dangerous child molester.

Besides the type of crime committed by offenders, two other criteria of dangerousness have received attention throughout this book. The risk to individual victims in particular and society in general also have been gauged by the criminal's record of recidivism which defines risk in terms of the number of victims claimed sequentially by the same man. In addition, the criminal's parole record offers evidence of incorrigibility, the failure to learn how to conform to the expectations of society or its institutions even when it means maintaining freedom from incarceration.

About 40% of the high-dangerousness group were recidivists with a history of repeated sex-crime, whereas only 12% of the low-dangerousness group were sex-crime recidivists ($p<.05$). Examination of parole records revealed that 43% of the high group had experienced problems on their most recent parole or actually had their paroles revoked. This compared with a 10% figure for the low-dangerousness group ($p<.01$). Both sets of figures testify to the less modifiable character of the highly-dangerous heterosexual child molester and the continuity of risk associated with his criminality. These findings, as well as the previous results regarding social class and intoxication, testify to the singular danger associated with high dangerousness when it is found in the man who molests girls. The mental disturbance suggested by prior psychometric analyses for these men may contribute to any or all of these additional risk-related variables.

Psychometric appraisal of disturbed thinking in ultradangerous

criminals. In what will be the final examination of evidence regarding the relationship between criminal dangerousness and mental disturbance, I will return to the study comparing NGRI patients who were not held responsible for their violent conduct and violent criminals who were punished for their crimes. You may recall that the results confirmed even greater dangerousness in the mentally-ill group than in violent prisoners. My conclusion was that the combination of dangerousness and the further impairment of mental illness presented an incremental risk of violence. The absence of a mentally-ill group with no violence in their backgrounds prevented an effort to verify this conclusion.

The sample of violent criminals within the NGRI investigation offered the opportunity to examine the dangerousness -- mental illness contingency more closely as far as its implications for violent conduct were concerned. More information was available for these prisoners than for the NGRI patients, including an assessment of their prison adjustment. The study also included a psychometric index for both the prisoners and patients that measured disturbed thinking, largely to confirm the mental disturbance implied by the NGRI verdict. This index of disturbed thinking was very similar to the psychotic tetrad used in the study reported earlier in this chapter except only three of the four MMPI tetrad scales were involved -- Paranoia, Psychasthenia, and Schizophrenia. These were taken to be indicators of anomalous thinking of a delusional, obsessive, or bizarre nature (among other things). Raw scale scores transformed to standard scores ($\underline{M}$=50, $\underline{SD}$=10) provided an index with a hypothetical mean of 150. This index confirmed the greater thought disturbance of the NGRI group ($\underline{M}$=177.78) relative to the violent criminals ($\underline{M}$=150.17, $\underline{p}$<.001) in the original study.

The conduct records of the 204 violent prisoners had been subjected to ratings on a behavioral scale that considered the violent or nonviolent nature of each prison violation; disciplinary reports were rated along a 7-point scale of increasing severity. Dividing the sample of prisoners into three levels of prison misconduct was achieved by defining low misconduct by cumulative ratings of 0 ($\underline{N}$=68), intermediate misconduct by cumulative ratings of 1-6($\underline{N}$=65), and high misconduct by rating totals of 7-101($\underline{N}$=71). When disturbed-thinking index scores were compared across these levels of misconduct, an association was noted: low misconduct = 146.54, intermediate misconduct = 147.56, and high misconduct = 156.04. However, the relationship between disturbed thinking and prison misconduct lacked statistical significance.

The point of these preliminary comments is that an ultradangerous criminal group can be identified within the sample of prisoners in the NGRI study, defined not only by the dangerousness index but also by two markers of violent antisocial conduct. All prisoners had committed violent crimes before they came to prison. Only about a third of these violent criminals gained the dubious distinction of being included in the highest tier of prison misconduct with cumulative rating scores that were so substantial as to almost require repeated violence or threatened violence in their records. Then add to these markers of past violence the further confirmation of dangerousness implicit in elevated index scores, and some degree of certainty regarding potential victim risk is warranted. Now the question remains whether the fourth piece of the risk picture will fall into place. Will the man committing a violent crime, follow this by becoming a serious (highest tier) conduct problem in prison, and then qualify as high (above the sample median) in dangerousness as defined by the model show up as singularly disturbed in his thought processes?

The answer to this question can be found in these results. The ultradangerous criminals ($\underline{N}$=48) obtained an average disturbed-thinking score of 162.92, far higher than that of the 23 men whose crime and prison conduct were of a more violent bent but who had lower (below-median) dangerousness index scores ($\underline{M}$=141.70, $\underline{p}$<.001). None of the between-group comparisons not involving the ultradangerous criminals attained statistical significance, and the mean disturbed-thinking scores ranged between 143.45 and 151.46. The conclusion here seems straightforward enough, although I will rearrange the variables under analysis in order to better make my point. Criminals who are defined by the model as dangerous and who combine these limitations with a singularly high thinking disturbance represent the most clearcut risk of violent conduct in the community and in prison.

Conclusion. In this chapter I have considered mental disorder and criminality from two perspectives as a way of addressing the issue of how mental illness may interface with criminal dangerousness. The NGRI analysis revealed that patients diagnosed as mentally disordered and not held responsible for their violent acts are more dangerous than violent prisoners who have done the same thing but were punished for their crimes. Several other studies disclosed a link between dangerousness and abnormal behavior in convicted criminals using scales measuring aberrant or diminished thought rather than psychiatric verdict as a criterion of disorder. Both sets of results convince me that the combination of dangerousness and mental abnormality promotes an increased risk for crime and violence than either taken alone. The most promising explanation for their combined effect within the theoretical model is that mental disorder contributes further to the cognitive anomalies and distortion of social values already represented in criminal dangerousness.

Section IV

Conclusions from the Research Program

Chapter 11

The Dangerousness Model: Scientific and Practical Implications

It is difficult to anticipate what the reaction will be to the program of research into criminal behavior in general and violence in particular described in the preceding chapters and to the theoretical model it has generated. The best I could hope for from the community of scholars, researchers, and professionals committed to the problems of crime and violence would be acceptance of the dangerousness model into the family of theories that seek to explain antisocial behavior. Given that kind of visibility, others may accept the challenge of establishing how the dangerousness model, as it stands, stacks up against other ways of explaining criminal activity or of refining the theoretical model that at this point represents only a basic blueprint.

The Scientific Perspective

The research that has been completed in our program suggests two things to me that should have a bearing upon how the evidence is regarded. The sheer volume of evidence consistent with the proposed dangerousness model makes it next to impossible to conclude that these ideas hold no merit. Perhaps the particular version of criminal risk that I have chosen to integrate the myriad findings may not prove to be totally on mark. However, if my multifactorial dangerousness notion is not totally appropriate, then some alternative explanation for the aggregate of significant findings is called for, one that provides a better theoretical fit. I think it would be a mistake to shrug off a cache of evidence bearing upon crime and violence just because the first theoretical approximation does not qualify as convincing.

The second observation that I would make regarding the research evidence collected in testing the dangerousness model ignores the dictates of humility altogether. What I really believe is that the procedures that have been followed and the weight of evidence should earn serious consideration for the specific personality-based interpretation of criminal risk that has been proposed. Strategy of research has included an effort to go beyond simply conducting a number of studies that are relevant to dangerousness but to insure that confidence in the theoretical model increases as the program progresses. To do this the research into criminal behavior has proceeded programmatically so that the results from earlier studies had a bearing upon the goals and methodology of studies to follow. This has resulted in a series of investigations that has provided a broad and integrated network of relationships. I also have sought to progressively refine the proof used to test the adequacy of the dangerousness proposal. As validation has made increasing demands upon the theoretical model, it has become more and more difficult to generate support. Since the evidence has met the test of progressive refinement, confidence in the proposal might be expected to increase exponentially.

One way in which increasing refinement of proof was accomplished evolved from my definition of dangerousness in terms of victim harm. It follows, then, that increments of dangerousness in the criminal should be found as crimes involving increases in harm to the victim are considered. This requirement spawned a series of studies in which the discrimination between criminal groups made increasing demands upon the model. The dangerousness index initially was shown to discriminate between two general classes of male criminals as violent offenders, acknowledged to be more dangerous and at greater risk of seriously harming their victims, were distinguished from less dangerous nonviolent offenders. The difference, while supporting the model, lacked the specificity to qualify as crucial. The focus of discrimination was subsequently refined by dangerousness comparisons between male criminals all of whom had committed some type of violent crime. Groupings of violent criminals, ordered by severity of violence, demonstrated the predicted order of dangerousness. Finally, the most serious forms of violence were subjected to within-crime analysis. Men who had perpetrated these crimes under especially heinous circumstances were compared to their criminal counterparts whose violence lacked the excesses of cruelty and social stigma. The predicted difference in dangerousness, based upon harm to the victim, was found when murderers alone were considered and, independently, within a group of rapists.

Another way in which the dangerousness model met the requirements of more demanding validation was in its ability to accommodate several criteria of criminal dangerousness rather than just one. While it was true that much of the evidence considered to be validational in nature involved discrimination between criminals whose offenses inflicted varying degrees of harm upon their victims, three other important markers of victim jeopardy were also examined. Criminal recidivism offered a different perspective on risk. Rather than addressing the severity of harm implicit in a given criminal act, repeated criminality emphasizes the danger of harm to a succession of victims. Recidivism, gauged by past record of felonies, almost always occurs despite incarceration and other efforts of society to deter continuing antisociality. Dangerousness was found to predict criminal recidivism.

Adjustment on parole allows yet another perspective on dangerousness with distinct differences from harmfulness of specific crimes or the tendency to repeat criminal activities. This criterion of dangerousness offers immediate feedback concerning whether incarceration has had a constructive impact upon the criminal's motivation/ability to live within a socially-regulated society, a society that lacks the simplistic code of conduct and immediate supervision found in prison. Prisoners who cannot meet parole expectations are more dangerous in my theoretical sense, because they have been less amenable to correction and sustain their potential for victim harm. The expectation that more dangerous criminals would perform less adequately under the transitional conditions of parole was confirmed for both men and women.

Finally, the criteria of dangerousness were extended into the realm of prison conduct on much the same rationale as that presented for parole adjustment. When efforts to modify the antisociality of the prisoner by punishment and rehabilitation are to less avail, evidenced by inability to satisfy the conduct code within the prison system, the criminal remains a greater risk to society upon reentry. Prison preparation of the prisoner for future regard of social rules and the rights of others was demonstrably less effective for the dangerous inmate who continued to demonstrate his antisocial ways by breaching the established conduct code. Misconduct in prison represented an especially ominous harbinger for future victim risk in this analysis, since it was recorded in such a way as to emphasize potential for violence.

Besides engaging a variety of criteria for criminal dangerousness, studies in the research program made both retrospective and prospective demands upon the theoretical model. Although most of the research data took the form of relationships between the dangerousness index and previous antisocial activity, there was ample demonstration of true predictive power for the model as prospective relationships were considered. All data analyses bearing upon parole outcome and one recidivism study that tracked criminals over a substantial number of years satisfied the requirements of true prediction. That dangerousness scores allowed some degree of prediction for a number of years after the measurements were taken lends further confidence to the viability of the model.   The fact that predictability of future crime was demonstrated even for lower baserate violence seems especially significant.

The essential feature of my particular theory of criminal dangerousness is that the potential for harming victims varies with the combined presence of antisociality and poor cognitive resources. The criminal motivation and lack of moral restraint associated with antisociality and a variety of cognitive flaws that would be expected given low intelligence not only make it more likely that crimes will be committed but also increase the likelihood that poor planning or faulty execution of the crime will be involved. The bungling criminal places the victim at greater risk of serious harm by poorly-conceived criminal activity and the failure to anticipate exigencies. Added to this once a crime is initiated, the bungler is less able to cope with unexpected complications that arise in criminal transaction.   The dangerous criminal, short on devising alternatives, judgment, interpersonal skills, and self-restraint, may be incapable of resolving the situation without resorting to violence or escalating the intended level of violence.

The two factors proposed as key to understanding dangerousness, antisociality and cognitive deficits, as well as the particular way in which they interact to increase the risk of harm to the victims of crime did not receive the detailed analysis that they require. The limited accessibility of prisoners themselves and reliance on file data made it difficult to seek new information from criminals on an individual basis that would be required in order to substantiate and elaborate the theoretical nuances of the dangerousness model. However, our studies did allow some examination of the assumptions that were critical to the methodology of investigation or that rest at the theoretical core of the model. This evidence showed the assumptions to be defensible and should be placed alongside validation by discrimination, multiple criteria of criminal risk, and future prediction of dangerous conduct as supporting the dangerousness proposal as it stands.

The assumptions in our research methodology had to do with the manner in which the two dangerousness factors were measured. Antisociality was never studied in isolation as a dangerousness factor, but the fact that our research had to depend upon two different approaches to measuring this variable adds to our confidence in the outcome. The evidence bearing upon the power of the model was equally positive whether antisociality was scored from a combination of personality scales or from the social history indicators of antisocial personality. Flawed cognition, which I believe will turn out to be a more complicated factor, did receive more direct attention.

Piecemeal evidence did substantiate the assumption that low IQ, as measured by a standard culture-free intelligence test, translates readily into impaired cognition as a source of faulty criminal planning and transaction. The dangerous criminal, as defined in part by lower intelligence, was found to be less effective in his thinking when personality scales were examined. The likelihood of diminished transactional skills in the dangerous criminal was suggested by lower sociability, limited psychological-mindedness, and less empathy. These would contribute to his difficulties in the social conduct of a crime that could place the victim at increased risk. Impaired self-control was found in the most dangerous criminals, helping to explain the criminality of the antisocial individual in the face of social deterrents to crime. It also offers insight into the deterioration of transactions with a victim for the dangerous criminal into unpremeditated violence as emotions promote harmful impulsive behavior.

The critical theoretical assumption of the model is that danger to the victims of crime stems in large measure from antisociality that promotes unlawful behavior and flawed cognition that elevates risk further by bungled planning and conduct of the crime. Confidence in this assumption was strengthened when disruptive state variables were identified that amplified the potential harm conferred by criminal dangerousness. Dangerous men were more likely to commit crimes while under some influence of alcohol or drugs. Alcohol might promote joviality in a bar and drugs might enhance sociality at a party. However, it seems inevitable that intoxication would impair the cognitive abilities of dangerous offenders, already suspect, as they anticipate the commission of a crime and conduct the criminal transaction. Cognitive impairment of the criminal promises only more harm for the victim of a crime. Much the same conclusion seems warranted in extrapolating from the finding that mentally ill men who engage in violence are more dangerous than ordinary violent criminals or that more dangerous violent criminals show evidence of thought disturbance. Mental disorder, like intoxication, augurs poorly for the victim as far as either planning and initiation of a crime or interpersonal transactions during a crime are concerned. This follows from the expectation that the flawed cognitive functioning associated with dangerousness would be further magnified by psychological disorder; deficits relevant to dangerous conduct would be more profound or more diverse.

Granting the dangerousness model some degree of credibility as an explanation for crime in general and criminal violence in particular still leaves open the question of how broadly this explanation may apply. Our statistical analyses, in line with the procedures of psychological science, routinely generated support for the theoretical model by examining group effects -- general trends in the data. The same evidence, however, make it clear that exceptions to the theory were anything but rare. Some men convicted of criminal violence presented relatively low dangerousness-index scores; other men for whom we could verify no history of violence at the time of assessment were designated as very dangerous by the index. The limited prediction (or postdiction) of behavior from psychological individual-difference variables is not rare. In fact, it is safe to say that psychology has yet to come up with an example of theory-based prediction of behavior, based upon psychometric or any other kind of data, that can meet the exacting standards of the natural sciences. Nevertheless, there are many reasons why limitations of the model may be more apparent than real in explaining dangerous criminality. Not the least of these is the fact that the dangerousness model is not a fully-articulated theory. The limits of its inherent predictive power remain vague at this point in time.

Another reason why the dangerousness model may appear less powerful than it might otherwise is that the analyses always involved comparisons between criminals, men and women who had proven themselves incapable of abiding by the legal rules that govern social conduct. This meant that discrimination, when that procedure was used as the means of validating the model, required differentiation between people who had criminality in common and, thus, a shared propensity to harm victims. It would have been much simpler to demonstrate a difference in dangerousness if criminals had been compared with men or women with no known history of criminal behavior. I would expect the contrast in dangerousness between law-abiding people and proven criminals to be especially striking.

Using noncriminals in our research program, if it had been logistically feasible, could have proven more important than just providing more emphatic results corroborating model validity. It could have allowed us to cast criminal dangerousness in a different light by extending our interest into the developmental origins of crime. The index score offers the opportunity to consider the potential for crime and violence in those who have not as yet engaged in serious antisociality, at least reaching back into the adolescent years. Identifying the risk of criminal violence before it occurs would offer the social scientist the opportunity to look for precipitating factors. On a more professional note, early identification would allow for programs of prevention to be introduced and evaluated before the confounding effects of repeated exposure to the criminal-justice system are registered.

While satisfying multiple criteria of dangerous criminality has been cited as a strongpoint of our research, there is a complication to this diversity that remains unexplored in terms of the current dangerousness model. In subjecting the four primary validating criteria to analysis, it became clear to me that more dangerous outcomes were not evidenced across the board when more than one criterion was examined for a given set of offenders. Male criminals who committed more serious crimes were not necessarily those who were recidivists, who failed to adjust on parole, or who were conduct problems in prison. Even though the index score was predictably related to all of these criteria, a man with a high dangerousness score was not likely to emerge as a risk in every way we considered. There was a hint of this in the female results as well when dangerousness was related to severity of criminal violence only after a complicated set of analyses involving several additional crime and offender variables. Yet parole outcome fell in line with expectations in a straightforward way for the same women.

That all types of criminally-dangerous behavior cannot be anticipated from the high index score of a given individual does not present an insurmountable problem, but it will require further progress in developing the dangerousness model. A search for greater specificity that will help identify the particular facet of dangerousness best predicted from a given high index score is in order. This could take the form of identifying new variables that interact with dangerousness to predict a particular dangerous outcome. It could just as readily involve a revised weighting system for antisociality and IQ depending upon which criterion is being considered. Should the future bring a more refined specification of what constitutes antisociality and flawed cognition, the solution could involve yet another form of weighting. For example, predicting severity of criminal acts might require one subset of cognitive deficiencies and predicting recidivism or parole outcome might depend upon a somewhat different pattern of cognitive limitations.

I suggested earlier in this chapter that the presence of "false-positive" and "false-negative" subjects in every study that I have reported gives the appearance of limited power for the dangerousness model. Some very dangerous criminals, as gauged by their index scores, had a history of only nonviolent crimes, and a few criminals with low dangerousness scores were guilty of very serious violence. These seeming errors of measurement could be explained in several ways without impugning the theoretical model. To begin with, the appearance of exceptions to theory could find explanation in some rather obvious facts of life for psychologists who are invested in constructing theories involving social behavior. Any theoretical model at an early stage of development is going to misfire simply because it is not fully formulated. In addition, the measurement of critical variables within the theory, required for validation, is imperfect. Mistakes in prediction may be made that have far less to do with theoretical validity than with imperfections in measuring and quantifying theoretical variables.

Another explanation for the glaring exceptions to theory that appear is that these misrepresented criminals might in some cases provide evidence for model validity if more were known. The false-negative case, where highly dangerous acts are perpetrated by criminals whose antisociality and IQ credentials argue for low dangerousness, could occur for any number of psychological reasons. Any set of conditions that results in an uncharacteristic and temporary departure from the individual's typical level of restraint may promote momentary risk of harming some victim. A lot of domestic violence involves men and women who would not otherwise be criminals and who would not look especially dangerous by the model index score. However, at the time that violence erupts, it would be safe to assume that the quality of cognitive function would be compromised by emotional arousal. By the same token, the restraining features of social values also would be expected to suffer in an emotional crisis so that at the moment of violence the perpetrator would be functionally antisocial. Standardized testing of value and cognition, intended to establish a potential for dangerous criminality, was not devised to reveal the risk of harmful behavior under episodic conditions of extreme emotionality.

A somewhat different explanation for dangerous behavior displayed by people who might appear benign if gauged by the dangerousness model would be in terms of group or ideological commitment that overrides typical modes of response. At one extreme, terrorist activities based upon political or religious views may result in wanton destructiveness and violence that would be unexpected from the same people if behaviors outside these domains of commitment were examined. When ideology assumes a paramount role in determining aggressive behavior, higher-level cognition will suffer and broadly-shared values will be lost. This is not to say that model-defined dangerousness will be unrepresented among terrorists. It does suggest that criminal dangerousness can be confined to an aspect of a person's life set apart by overzealous belief. The abortion-rights issue has spawned its own examples of criminality based upon the compromise of cognition and values implicit in rigid commitment to a particular view. Pro-life activists would not likely appear dangerous by my measurement procedures, but they are responsible for purposeful crimes extending to serious violence.

The other type of gross measurement error observed in our research data was the very dangerous criminal by model standards who had committed only property crimes that are relatively harmless to the victim compared to violent offenses. The false-positive case attracts a different kind of explanation if the error is to be considered more apparent than real. The failure of highly dangerous criminals, as defined by the model, to have been convicted of more dangerous (violent) crimes at the point they were studied may have had more to do with the number of crimes that remain unsolved by the police or with other imperfections in criminal justice than with faulty measurement. Criminal history was always considered, but a crime must be solved and a conviction rendered before it becomes a part of anyone's record.

The fact that a given individual marked by high dangerousness scores may not as yet have encountered the circumstances that are conducive to violence in a criminal situation also is a possibility. This and other explanations for false-positive measurement errors received some backing from evidence generated in our research program. The argument that given time the highly dangerous criminal will confirm his risk status by serious harm to a crime victim was put to test in the long-term prospective study of recidivism. By following the criminal behavior of prisoners from 3 to 21 years following assessment of dangerousness and subsequent release from prison allowed us to consider what happened when nonviolent criminals were allowed time to recidivate. Those who did not engage in violence, including 30 who returned to nonviolent crime and 13 who remained crime-free, showed a low dangerousness score on the average. The nine prisoners who had displayed only nonviolent offenses when they were assessed but eventually ended up convicted of criminal violence were highly dangerous at the time measurement was made (about 600 points higher) and qualified as false-positive at that point. The model proved prophetic, but it took time. The same long-term study cast light on the false-negative case as well; violent criminals who did not return to violent crime were low on the dangerousness score to begin with.

The truth of the matter is that I do not believe that our data should hit the mark across a wide spectrum of criminals, even in principle. The psychological explanation for criminal dangerousness in its various guises offered in this book is not expected to have universal application. I think that progress in understanding the psychological basis for criminal behavior will reveal several critical antecedent conditions that predispose the individual to violence and other harmful criminal actions. The relative importance of these explanations of criminal conduct and their relationship to one another will be a matter for future determination. Once psychological explanation is brought into sharper focus, the social/cultural and biological parameters of crime can be more rigorously determined as co-determinants of antisocial conduct.

To this point I have emphasized the validating consistencies in the evidence generated by studies in our research program -- the varied criteria and correlates of criminal dangerousness that fell into place when the theoretical model was tested. There also were some characteristics of the criminal that threatened to complicate the application of the model. These characteristics -- gender, race, and mental status -- when analyzed at greater length proved to be promising ways of refining the dangerousness model and expanding its explanatory value rather than obstacles to validation.

The gender difference in dangerousness was most evident in the predictiveness of the index score for both women and men for one criterion but less so for another. Dangerous criminals of both sexes showed poorer outcomes on parole. However, the systematic tendency for increasingly more dangerous men to commit ever-more-severe violent crimes was not found in women, at least in an uncomplicated way. Although female violent criminals, like their male counterparts, were higher in criminal dangerousness than their nonviolent counterparts in an earlier study, the fact that discrimination was erratic between severity levels of violence in the more rigorous follow-up investigation of female criminals encourages me to take the gender difference seriously.

There is ample evidence in the criminal literature to understand why female violence might require a different explanation than is the case for men. I cited two studies (Heilbrun, 1982; Heilbrun & Heilbrun, 1986) earlier in this book that cast some light upon female violence and the gender issue in dangerousness. The 1982 study confirmed that women committed crimes involving physical violence more by impulse than was true for their male counterparts. Even though violent crimes are generally more impulsive than property crimes for everybody, female criminals still demonstrated an ultra-impulsive character to their acts of physical aggression. This distinct level of impulsivity was not evident when property crimes were examined or even violent crime lacking actual physical aggression; women were actually more premeditated in offenses of this nature than men. Accordingly, we can assume that female impulsivity pertains only to the expression of physical violence and not to criminal conduct in general.

The 1986 follow-up study confirmed that the courts had taken cognizance of the discrepancy in impulsive violence between women and men in post-feminism years by more proper calibration of sentences in line with the impulsivity or premeditation of the criminal act. Women, more impulsive than men in the commission of physical violence, were extended more lenient sentences as before. On the other hand, nonviolent crimes attracted average sentences for women and men that were very similar, departing from earlier lenient sentencing for females.

The failure of the dangerousness model to relate systematically to severity of violence when women were subjected to study was interpreted in the light of these two studies. Women show inhibitions regarding the expression of physical aggression; violence, when it does occur, is generally going to be a spur-of-the-moment act. The dangerous woman may well be vulnerable to escalating violence during confrontational criminal situations because of flawed cognition, much like the dangerous male, but she is also prey to emotion-driven impulsivity. However, the impulsivity of dangerous women is probably matched in less dangerous women when emotions are aroused. If so, women, dangerous or not, can be brought to the point of impulsive physical aggression by the overriding emotions of the moment. This would tend to diminish the differences in violence potential between women varying in criminal dangerousness and blur the model as it was found to apply to men.

I think it is important to point out that the deviation from the model in the violence domain was related exclusively to the female murderer whose dangerousness scores failed to reflect the seriousness of her crime and the harm done to her victim. Mid-severity violence like assault did fall in place theoretically as women convicted of this crime revealed far greater dangerousness than low-severity criminals who harmed victims through violence but without intent. Even with female murderers, consideration of victim characteristics brought improved alignment with the specifications of the model. Women who suffered a history of abuse by a particular male and subsequently killed him revealed little in the way of dangerousness; they would appear to be prime candidates as murderers by emotion-driven impulse. If only women and children are considered as the victims of murder, the violence-severity findings fell fully in place for the white women who killed but the black female murderer still proved to be a problem for the model. My conclusion in light of these results on violence and the background research is that the gender difference in model applicability stems from the greater complexity in explaining murder by women in today's America.

The data made it clear that the dangerousness model was capable of anticipating difficulties on parole for more dangerous women. This seems to be explained most simply by the fact that problems on parole go well beyond committing a new crime, especially beyond violent recidivism. Ratings of parole adjustment in women made note of problems in conforming to parole conditions or actual technical violations of these conditions in 57% of the cases where parole was not progressing satisfactorily. The remaining 43% of parole difficulties involved criminal recidivism, but only 4% of the crimes were of a violent nature. Murder, the crime that introduced such complications in model validation for women, was unrepresented among these few violent crimes and could play no role in attenuating model effectiveness. Parole conduct tells us a great deal about antisocial attitudes, motivation to stay out of prison, and ability to accommodate to regulations. However, emotionality and subsequent impulsive aggression seems to play no substantive role in determining women's success or failure. The dangerousness model works better with parole prediction, because emotions are unlikely to make less dangerous women momentarily act like more dangerous women and kill someone within this period of conditional release.

The issue of whether criminal dangerousness varies by race presented its own brand of complications. The answer, based upon program evidence, depends upon whether dangerousness is considered as a shared racial characteristic, as a theoretical construct, or as a dynamic of criminal-victim interaction during a crime. The answer to the first possibility would certainly be that black criminals were more dangerous than white within my theoretical scheme of things if dangerousness is examined strictly in terms of group averages for the two races. An observation that is bound to be made given this finding is whether it may have resulted from some bias in our research methodology or in the Georgia criminal justice system that provided subjects for our investigations. Although it is possible that bias may have been operative in some way as to improperly cast black criminals as presenting a higher risk of harm to the victims of their crimes, it is difficult for me to imagine that the effect is strictly an artifact of method and availability.

To start with, I do not take the "culture-bound" concerns about the intelligence and personality testing of white and black subjects very seriously as these have surfaced over the years. Race-specific testing procedures have not been demonstrated to be that critical. Our measurement procedures do not seem to be the place to start in isolating racial bias for other reasons as well. The IQ test was developed to be free of racial bias, and the personality measures were often replaced by case history information without changing the trend of higher black dangerousness scores.

It is always possible that black offenders are treated differently at one stage or another within the criminal justice system resulting in an unrepresentative black prison population from which we drew our subjects. Bias could creep in in terms of who gets arrested, convicted, or paroled so that black criminals come to selectively differ from their white counterparts in prison. The problem with an argument that racial bias resulted in an unrepresentative black population in prison, at least as far as the dangerousness evidence was concerned, is that the contention would lend itself to the wrong conclusion. If too many blacks are in prison for reasons other than their dangerous predisposition, it would lead me to expect the relative dangerousness of our black subjects to be lower than that of white criminals. Just the opposite finding was routinely observed; black prisoners had higher dangerousness scores. The disproportionality of blacks in the Georgia prison system is matched by their generally more dangerous predisposition.

If the research evidence is examined in a different way, race is shown to be unimportant to the understanding of criminal dangerousness. The relationships by which we validated the model or extended its network of correlates were essentially identical for black and white criminals. Said another way, the "laws" of dangerous potential were the same whether black or white offenders were considered. Racial differences in the relationships encompassed by the model were found primarily when more focused analysis was introduced that considered interracial transaction in the course of violent crime.

As attention was turned to criminal transaction between male criminals and victims of either sex, the pendulum again swung to the obvious importance of race in understanding dangerousness and harm to the victim of a crime. The evidence here pointed toward brutal excesses of violence by the more dangerous black criminal under two conditions. The murder of white victims by black murderers tended to attract the death penalty; at the same time, closer examination of the crimes revealed the exceptional cruelty that often serves as the basis for this verdict as well as the highest level of dangerousness in the murderer. Black men who killed black victims were not exceptional as far as receiving the death penalty or in their dangerousness. A comparable finding was observed when the actual circumstances of rape were examined. Ratings of the criminal acts reflected more harmful treatment of the white female victim, both psychologically and physically, by the more dangerous black rapist. When the black rapist victimized a black woman, no comparable effect of dangerousness was observed.

Interracial violence committed by white criminals was rare. In the death-penalty study the incidence of white-on-black murder was too infrequent to even analyze. Later search of Parole Board files suggested that our initial sampling was not unrepresentative of serious violent crime; whites infrequently raped black women, although they were frequently responsible for victimizing white women. The value of considering the racial pattern provided by the violent criminal and his victim in calibrating the dangerousness model is selective. Dangerousness is important in predicting harmful extremes only when the criminal is black and the victim is white.

I have suggested that the dangerous black criminal who engages in violence toward white victims may do so with extraordinary vehemence in part because of an underlying resentment and hostility toward those who are perceived as the source of their social disadvantagement. By the same token, the amount of harm to the victim is generally proportional to the amount of resistance that the victim offers; the criminal's aggression and the victim's resistance to aggression are mutually dependent. The offender may increase his aggression as his criminal goals are opposed by victim resistance; victim resistance may increase as concern about personal survival or resentment about criminal aggression mounts. When this kind of mutual escalation takes place, the brutality of the final act of violence is likely to increase. This would be especially likely if the dangerousness of the criminal accelerated the interaction of force and resistance by his transactional limitations or other consequences of flawed cognition or antisociality. In the special case of the black violent criminal and the white victim, preexisting attitudes toward whites may add even further to the brutality if the offender is dangerous enough.

Some of the resistance that whites demonstrate to being victimized by black criminals may have its origins in the victims' racial prejudices, stereotypes, and fears related to race. To be attacked by a black criminal may seem especially out of keeping with early precedents governing social conduct of the two races in this country. This would be most evident in the early proscription against the sexual approach of a black man toward a white woman. It would be difficult for the intended female victim not to have some glimmering of this interracial legacy so that black-on-white rape would provoke even greater fear and aversion than intraracial rape. Should the white victim react in a more vigorous way to protect herself in resisting the dangerous black rapist, these vestiges of special interracial bias would further increase her risk of harm. Unfortunately for the victim, our data showed that if the black rapist is highly dangerous, it does not make much difference. The white victim will suffer more brutal treatment if she resists or not. It is only a matter of degree.

Each set of findings regarding the role of race in understanding criminal dangerousness holds some importance for theoretical development of the model. That black criminals show up as more dangerous than white offers the opportunity to understand black crime, especially black violence, in terms of personal attributes rather than social or cultural developmental context. While these background conditions are certainly critical determinants of criminal attributes, it is the personal attribute that promises a more malleable target for change. The common ground between white and black criminals, as far as the relationships between dangerousness and crime are concerned, is no less important. As we learned years ago when construct validation of measures was in vogue, there is value in knowing which relationships do not hold as well as which do when we are trying to establish whether a measure is performing according to theory. It is of value knowing that in many ways black and white dangerousness lends itself to the same behavior. The implications of criminal-victim race might be thought of as the most important disclosure as far as theory is concerned. They offer an articulation of the model that might otherwise remain buried in the specific circumstances of violent crime, overlooked as possibilities in the issues of race, crime, and punishment.

The third issue involving the possible interface of a demographic characteristic with the relationship between dangerousness and victim harm adds yet another wrinkle to the theoretical model. The question here concerned whether mental disorder contributed one way or another to the risk of harming victims of crime. When men who were judged to be mentally ill at the time of committing some violent act (and not held accountable for their violence) were compared to similarly violent men in prison, the mentally-ill men proved to be more dangerous by index score. This suggests to me, on the one hand, that violence in men who are suffering a mental disorder has comparable origins to any other criminal violence -- in the reciprocal effects of antisociality and cognitive limitation. This particular sample of mentally-disordered men, who had engaged in dangerous aggressive conduct, displayed the same instigation to crime and violence through dangerousness as did violent criminals in prison, even more. If we ask the question whether the mentally ill are a special risk for violence, these results alone would not serve as proof that they are. If we ask whether dangerous mentally-ill men are a risk, the answer would be in the affirmative. Short of having concordance rates between dangerousness and mental disorder or mental disorder and violence, about all I could say following this line of reasoning is that mental illness does not introduce anything new to the model except that the mentally disordered are not exempt from the effects of dangerousness.

On the other hand, if you examine the evidence from a different perspective, an added caveat regarding mental illness, dangerousness, and violence is in order. Someone showing a mental disorder as well as the limited intelligence implicit in high dangerousness is going to suffer extensive and profound cognitive deficits. More than that, antisocial values could be even further alienated from the mainstream by the disturbed thinking that is such a prominent feature of serious mental illness. In theory, these combined effects should generate a greater risk of violence as the psychological components of dangerousness are magnified. Mental disorders would be important for the theoretical model if it proved to be the case that dangerous men who are also mentally ill are even more of a risk for violence.

Discussing scientific considerations of the dangerousness research might best conclude by offering some suggestions concerning where this line of investigation should go next. It is not that the research methodology has been so rigorous or the theoretical model developed so complete as to narrow the possibilities particularly. My choice, however, if it were strenuously pursued, could very well hasten the time when the dangerousness model could put individual prediction of dangerous criminality on a sound footing.

Given the opportunity to go where I liked with dangerousness research as well as the logistical support that would be required, I would focus upon improved specification of antisociality patterns and cognitive limitations beyond the crude markers we have employed to date. Specific research questions regarding antisociality might start with whether the more critical feature is the absence of the values that promote prosocial behavior (e.g., honesty, respect for others' rights, constraint of physical aggression) or the presence of other values that promote antisocial behavior (e.g., egocentrism, machismo)? Besides clarifying whether antisociality is best understood in broad terms of constructive values that are missing or an abundance of negative values (or both), the relative importance of specific values needs to be resolved. The question here is whether there is a hierarchy of values, present or absent, that are important in fostering or deterring antisocial conduct? This would be especially important to answer in considering the criminal's convictions regarding physical aggression. I have emphasized the role of flawed cognition and lack of transactional skills in explaining criminal violence. The absence of moral restraint regarding physical aggression or, worse, a sadistic satisfaction in victim suffering would add tremendously to the risk posed by dangerousness.

Identifying which flawed cognitive skills or styles are critical to criminality and violence has received some attention in our research as diminished self-control, empathy, and psychological-mindedness along with poor utilization of available intellectual resources have been associated with higher dangerousness. Other psychometric indicators of disturbed or ineffective thinking in dangerous prisoners were identified, but they tended to be nonspecific. Whatever cognitive functions underlie social transaction were indirectly indicted when sociability was found lacking in the dangerous criminal. Many additional types of specific cognitive deficit remain to be investigated, especially those that would allow or even promote incompetent planning and transactional violence in the commission of a crime. This cognitive research must not only spread the net more broadly for flaws and search for patterns of impairment but must introduce improved measurement procedures. This would almost certainly require individual assessment using measures that have been developed as specific metrics of cognition. IQ scores were enough to get me this far in developing the dangerousness model, largely, in my opinion, because the theory was ripe for confirmation. However, future elaboration of this theoretical model will increasingly depend upon more precise cognitive measures that have been constructed to get at specific functions.

Let me assure any reader who maintains a career interest in scientific inquiry that the preceding admonitions regarding the ideal in future research represent something more than the pro forma signature statement of many scientific monographs; more investigation is necessary, but it must be of a more elaborate nature. More elegant procedures are not necessary to capitalize on what remains undiscovered. The evidence presented in this book, with positive results appearing in one study after another, suggests otherwise. The research offers a methodological framework by which the theoretical model could continue to be tested and expanded which is straightforward, logistically feasible if one has access to convicted criminals, and which certainly has proven effective enough to this point. Use the multiplicative index based on intelligence estimate and one of the antisociality measures to isolate a group of especially dangerous criminals, perhaps complementing the score by a proven history of violence, a poor conduct record in prison, or previous problems on parole. Devise a control group by requiring low index scores along with the absence of any other defining criterion of dangerousness. Then simply compare the two groups on whatever measures of social value or cognition that appear promising as a way of understanding criminal choice and violent outcome.

The most challenging aspect of future research will be to establish a measurement procedure that would allow for patterned personality differences to be identified to the extent they are found to be associated with the presence or absence of criminal dangerousness. The extremes of risk in criminals might be distinguished by the concomitant presence or absence of several traits, and a presence/absence pattern could turn out to be an important correlate of dangerousness and an avenue to elaborating theory. To state the obvious, you cannot identify patterned results unless the ingredients of the pattern are available in the investigation.

The Practical Perspective

The ultimate "moment-of-truth" for any program of study is when the practical significance of the findings and conclusions is considered. Statistical significance will inform the scientist about the probability that the results can be reproduced by someone else or occurred by chance. Ecological significance, the extent to which the research procedures are actually representative of some intended counterpart in the real world outside the laboratory, must be established by a blend of logic, common-sense, and scientifically-inspired reasoning. Practical significance is a different matter. Even granting the reliability and realistic quality of a discovery, does it make any contribution to the human condition? To put the issue baldly, so what? While there are some sciences that may not be judged on their contribution to contemporary humankind, this certainly should not be the case for social sciences such as psychology.

Judgment regarding the practical significance of the dangerousness model and the research upon which it is based might begin with a general observation about contemporary crime, especially violent crime. Even casual exposure to the popular news media confirms illegal behavior as a leading public concern, perhaps heading the list. That criminality in this country deserves such concern was confirmed by recent (August, 1995) statistics from the Justice Department, cited in the newspapers, that over 5,000,000 Americans were incarcerated or on probation or parole as convicted criminals.

I would argue, in fact, that more serious violent crimes represent an even greater dilemma than is portrayed by the popular media. A trend in the quality and quantity of violent behavior suggests that the problem of containing violence is even greater than the public is led to believe, because the various strands of aggression are rarely tied together to provide a comprehensive picture. The rate of violent crimes is often cited in terms of one statistic or another as evidence that preventive efforts are succeeding or failing or as violence capitals of the United States are crowned. At the same time, however, we are exposed to increasing numbers of multiple killings/assaults under circumstances where violence serves no obvious purpose other than mindless symbolism or personal vendetta. Male physical abuse of children or women is being revealed as a common theme in the continuing erosion of the family or other domestic arrangements and violent retaliation by the abused seems to be on the increase. Faced with these concerns at home, we also share an awareness of wholesale slaughter elsewhere in the world that occurs in the name of government, ethnic origin, or religion.

Even the fact that the dangerousness research was embedded within an area of critical social concern does not automatically mean that it disclosed much of practical significance, however. A legitimate claim to importance could be made if the discoveries held promise of accomplishing two things. The first of these would involve an improvement in our ability to make predictions of dangerous criminal behavior. There should be a discernible increase in accuracy of prediction with a firmer guarantee that errors would be held to an acceptable level. As the evidence stands at this point, the dangerousness index could prove useful for professional situations in which gross discrimination was required between criminals who were lower or higher risks of dangerous conduct.

Violent crimes, creating problems while incarcerated, violating the restrictions of parole, or criminal recidivism are to be expected of men who provide high index scores. It follows that designating more dangerous criminals as in collective need of special concern could prove of benefit to the criminal justice system at any phase of decision-making in which a choice of conditions is possible or even mandatory. This could include courtroom verdicts (as when mental disorder is involved), choice between prison or probation, assignments of prison status by security level, consideration for parole, or mass-release decisions. Any choice-point where it would be advantageous to know who is likely to present a risk to others within a succession of criminals would be a candidate for dangerousness measurement.

Examined from the vantage point of individual prediction of dangerous behavior rather than gross group discrimination, there is no doubt that the dangerousness model would make errors of prediction on a case to case basis despite improving matters in the longer run. An error might simply appear more glaring if considered alone. The importance of these individual errors when weighed against long-term benefits is a matter of professional judgment. It depends upon what actions follow upon the prediction and the relative cost of errors to the system, the public, and to the individual for whom the prediction is made.

If the contingent decision is of major significance (e.g., whether the criminal should be incarcerated or placed upon probation), the current capability for only gross group discrimination in level of dangerousness might encourage a conservative approach such as using only extreme dangerousness scores to help in the decision.   If, alternatively, the decision based upon the quantitative index is to involve less extreme alternatives (e.g., type of prison assignment, how closely parole should be monitored), I think there should be less concern about errors in individual prediction. The cost-versus-gain balance would have to be judged at each choice-point in which dangerousness scores are introduced as one basis for decision. Calibration by scoring extremes at a given choice-point is always a possibility.

There is another aspect to be considered in weighing the current practical significance of the dangerousness model as a predictor of future dangerous conduct. What other alternatives are available to the beleaguered criminal justice system?   Are there other empirically validated methods currently available for identifying individual criminals who are more likely to prove incorrigible in prison, irresponsible on parole, or recidivistic in their criminal behavior, especially when it comes to violence?   If there is still room for improvement in the early identification of potential problem cases, narrowing down the number of criminals requiring special concern by discrimination into more and less dangerous should prove worthwhile.

The dangerousness model could prove to have practical significance in another way.   It appears capable of identifying dangerous-appearing individuals at a time when efforts to modify their behavior would be more feasible.   It is not enough that the model allows some degree of prediction regarding who is at greater risk for crime and violence or other misconduct as planning becomes necessary regarding placement, supervision, or release from prison. The same model can be used to select criminals within a prison setting who are especially dangerous and for whom some form of intervention is called for to reduce future risk. The number of candidates for intervention could be adjusted by choosing score thresholds that provided realistic numbers.   Isolating the upper quartile of prisoner scores proved effective in predicting future criminality in the prospective study I reported.   The actual absolute value for identifying a need for intervention would depend upon the dangerousness norms that were used.

It is not that prisons are currently ignoring rehabilitation interventions that intend to accomplish the modification of risk for future dangerous conduct. Group programs geared to induce good citizenship, to improve emotional control or self-understanding, improve work skills, combat addiction to drugs and alcohol and so on are in place. However, the success of present approaches, as they must contend with the massive numbers of prisoners incarcerated in the United States, is questionable judging by rates of criminal recidivism. It is too easy for the prisoner to superficially conform to program goals as a way of building a prison record that encourages parole. The motivational conditions are not right to expect the more dangerous criminal to change in any important way.

If dangerousness, as specified by the model, was to become the focus of prison intervention, I could envision two levels of approach once that prime candidates for risk reduction are identified. At the less ambitious level, strategies of intervention, if ingeniously devised, could be put into place without introducing a new brand of skilled professionals into the prison system. There must be ways of working towards constructive values, better self-control, empathy, planfulness, and social-transactional skills, to mention only a few cognitive/social deficits contributing to dangerousness, without requiring a new kind of rehabilitation specialist. After all, prisons (along with mental hospitals) represent the ultimate in controlled environments. Modifying these environments for certain individuals earmarked as particularly dangerous should be possible as long as the modifications do not violate the general mandates of security and incarceration as punishment. If this approach proved promising or if resources allowed, specialists then could be trained to take on the interventions into dangerousness on a more demanding individual basis. Ingenuity would still be required to devise modification procedures for antisociality and cognitive flaws, but individual attention should improve the chances of successful intervention. The limits of expectation must be kept in mind, considering that low-IQ criminals who do not utilize even their limited intelligence very well are being targeted for improvement. This would be a consideration no matter whether the less or more ambitious approach to intervention were taken. Most importantly, I do not foresee these modification specialists, if they came to be employed, as being yet another version of psychotherapists. Intervention would not involve delving into personal problems in the traditional sense. It would be more a matter of training to improve deficiencies in value and cognition that promise to create problems for other people.

There is no reason why the principles of dangerousness confirmed by our research program could not ultimately prove valuable in deterring crime before it becomes a reality and exacts its cost for society and the offending individual. The psychological factors that may be recognized as part of an expanding dangerousness pattern -- antisociality, flawed cognition, and hesitant social behavior -- could become the foci of attention in children and adolescents before they become problematic delinquents and long before they end up as criminal adults in the penal system. The form and content of the measurement procedures would require some age-graded modifications, but the factors involved might well remain the same. The requirements of selection through measurement at younger ages are the same as when the objects of concern are adult criminals. It would be necessary to restrict numbers considerably before intervention procedures could be introduced, especially if individual strategies were to be employed. There is little use in trying to intervene with those who do not require that kind of help even if it were not impractical.

The best part of this proposal regarding early intervention is that the kind of modifications necessary to reduce the risk of future violence and criminality are, without exception, constructive alterations in behavior introduced at a time when the individual is most amenable to learning.

References

Adler, F. (1975) Sisters in crime. McGraw-Hill: New York.

American Psychiatric Association. (1968) Diagnostic and statistical manual of mental disorders (2nd ed.). Author: Washington, D.C.

Arieti, S. (1967) The intrapsychic self. Basic Books: New York.

Armstrong, G. (1977) Females under law -- protected but unequal. Crime and Delinquency, 23, 109-120.

Baldus, D.C., Pulaski, C., & Woodworth, G. (1983) Comparative review of death sentences: An empirical study of the Georgia experience. Journal of Criminal Law and Criminology, 74, 661-753.

Blackburn, R. (1975) An empirical classification of psychopathic personality. British Journal of Psychiatry, 127, 456-460.

Blackburn, R. (1979) Psychopathy and personality: The dimensionality of self-report and behavior rating data in abnormal offenders. British Journal of Social and Clinical Psychology, 18, 111-119.

Brizer, D.A., & Crowner, M. (1989) Current approaches to the prediction of violence. American Psychiatric Press: Washington, D.C.

Buck, J.A., & Graham, J.R. (1978) The 4-3 MMPI profile type: A failure to replicate. Journal of Consulting and Clinical Psychology, 46, 344.

Campbell, A. (1986) Self-report of fighting by females. The British Journal of Criminology, 26, 28-46.

Cattell, R.B., & Cattell, A.K.S. (1958) IPAT Culture Free Intelligence Test. Institute of Personality and Ability Testing: Champaign, IL.

Cattell, R.B., Feingold, S.N., & Sarason, S.B. (1941) A culture-free test of intelligence: II. Evaluation of cultural influence on test performance. Journal of Educational Psychology, 2, 81-100.

Chesney-Lind, M. (1977) Judicial paternalism and the female status offender. Crime and Delinquency, 23, 121-130.

Cleckley, H. (1964) The mask of sanity (4th ed.). Mosby: St. Louis, MO.

Craft, M.J. (1965) Ten studies into psychopathic personality. Wright: Bristol, England.

Dahlstrom, W.G., & Welsh, G.S. (1960) An MMPI handbook: A guide to use in clinical practice and research. University of Minnesota Press: Minneapolis.

Davis, K.R., & Sines, J.O. (1971) An antisocial behavior pattern associated with a specific MMPI profile. Journal of Consulting and Clinical Psychology, 36, 229-234.

Edinger, J.D. (1979) Cross-validation of the Megargee MMPI typology for prisoners. Journal of Consulting and Clinical Psychology, 47, 234-242.

Ervin, F., & Lion, J. (1969) Clinical evaluation of the violent patient. In D. Mulvihill & M. Tumin (Eds), Crimes of Violence: Staff report submitted to the National Commission on the Causes and Prevention of Violence. Vol. 13. U.S. Printing Office, Washington, D.C.

Feighner, J.P., Robins, E., Guze, S.B., Woodruff, R.A., Winokur, G., & Munoz, R. (1972) Diagnostic criteria for use in psychiatric research. Archives of General Psychiatry, 26, 57-63.

Foulds, G.A. (1965) Personality and personal interests. Tavistock: London.

Gebhard, P.H. (1965) Sex offenders. Harper: New York.

Goldstein, J.H. (1965) Aggression and crimes of violence. Oxford University Press: New York.

Gough, H.G. (1957) Manual for the California Psychological Inventory. Consulting Psychologists Press: Palo Alto, CA.

Gough, H.G. (1994) Theory, development, and interpretation of the CPI Socialization Scale. Psychological Reports, Monograph Supplement 1-75, 651-700.

Gunn, J. (1973) Violence. Praeger: New York.

Gynther, M.D., Altman, A., & Warbin, R.W. (1973) A new actuarial - empirical automated MMPI interpretive program: The 4-4/3-4 code type. Journal of Clinical Psychology, 29, 229-231.

Hare, R.D. (1970) Psychopathy: Theory and research. Wiley : New York.

Hare, R.D. (1978) Psychopathy and violence. Paper presented at the Symposium on Violence and the Violent Individual, Texas Research Institute of Mental Sciences, Houston, TX.

Hathaway, S.R., & McKinley, J.C. (1951) Manual for the Minnesota Multiphasic Personality Inventory (Rev. ed.). University of Minnesota Press: Minneapolis.

Heilbrun, A.B. (1978) Race, criminal violence, and length of parole. The British Journal of Criminology, 18, 53-61.

Heilbrun, A.B. (1979) Psychopathy and violent crime. Journal of Consulting and Clinical Psychology, 47, 509-516.

Heilbrun, A.B. (1982) Cognitive models of criminal violence based upon intelligence and psychopathy levels. Journal of Consulting and Clinical Psychology, 50, 546-557. (a)

Heilbrun, A.B. (1982) Female criminals: Behavior and treatment within the criminal justice system. Criminal Justice and Behavior, 9, 341-351. (b)

Heilbrun, A.B. (1990) The measurement of criminal dangerousness as a personality construct: Further validation of a research index. Journal of Personality Assessment, 54, 141-148. (a)

Heilbrun, A.B. (1990) Differentiation of death-row murderers and life-sentence murderers by antisociality and intelligence measures. Journal of Personality Assessment, 54, 617-627. (b)

Heilbrun, A.B., Foster, A., & Golden, J. (1989) The death sentence in Georgia 1974-1987. Criminal justice or racial injustice? Criminal Justice and Behavior, 16, 139-154.

Heilbrun, A.B., & Gottfried, D.M. (1988) Antisociality and dangerousness in women before and after the women's movement. Psychological Reports, 62, 37-38.

Heilbrun, A.B., & Heilbrun, K.S. (1977) The black minority criminal and violent crime: The role of self-control. The British Journal of Criminology, 17, 370-377.

Heilbrun, A.B., Heilbrun, L.C., & Heilbrun, K.L. (1978) Impulsive and premeditated homicide: An analysis of subsequent parole risk of the murderer. Journal of Criminal Law and Criminology, 69, 108-114.

Heilbrun, A.B., & Heilbrun, M.R. (1985) Psychopathy and dangerousness: Comparison, integration and extension of two psychopathic typologies. British Journal of Clinical Psychology, 24, 181-195.

Heilbrun, A.B., & Heilbrun, M.R. (1986) The treatment of women within the criminal justice system: An inquiry into the social impact of the women's rights movement. Psychology of Women Quarterly, 10, 240-251.

Heilbrun, A.B., & Heilbrun, M.R. (1989) Dangerousness and legal insanity. The Journal of Psychiatry and Law, Spring.

Heilbrun, A.B., Knopf, I.J., & Bruner, J. (1976) Criminal impulsivity and violence and subsequent parole outcome. The British Journal of Criminology, 16, 367-377.

Heilbrun, M.R. (1986) Not guilty by reason of insanity: An empirical test of the validity of the insanity verdict in the American criminal justice system. Senior honors thesis, Emory University.

Hoffman-Bustamente, D. (1973) The nature of female criminality. Issues in Criminality, 8, 117-136.

Hogan, R. (1969) Development of an empathy scale. Journal of Consulting and Clinical Psychology, 33, 307-316.

Hollmann, C.M. (1990) A comparison of heterosexual rapists and child molesters with special reference to the role of dangerousness. Senior honors thesis, Emory University.

Jastak, J.F., & Jastak, S.R. (1965) Wide Range Achievement Test Manual (Rev. ed.). Guidance Associates of Delaware: Wilmington.

Jensen, A.R. (1972) Review of the WLW Culture Fair Inventory. In O.K. Buros (Ed), The Seventh Mental Measurement Yearbook (Vol. 1). Gryphon Press: New York.

Karpman, B. (1961) The structure of neurosis: With special differentials between neurosis, psychosis, homosexuality, alcoholism, psychopathy, and criminality. Archives of Criminal Psychodynamics, 4, 599-646.

Katz, J.L. (1987, July 5) Death penalty data dispute racial bias claims. The Atlanta Journal and Constitution.

Kozel, H., Boucher, R., & Garofalo, R. (1972) The diagnosis and treatment of dangerousness. Crime and Delinquency, 18, 371-392.

Levy, S., Southcombe, R.H., Cranor, J.R., & Freeman, R.A. (1952) The outstanding personality factors among the population of a state penitentiary: A preliminary report. Journal of Clinical Experimental Psychopathology, 13, 117-130.

McCord, W., & McCord, J. (1964) The psychopath: An essay on the criminal mind. Van Nostrand: New York.

Megargee, E. (1976) The prediction of dangerous behavior. Criminal Justice and Behavior, 3, 3-21.

Mischel, W. (1973) Toward a cognitive social learning reconceptualization of personality. Psychological Review, 80, 252-283.

Monahan, J. (1975) The prediction of violence. In D. Chappell & J. Monahan (eds), Violence and criminal justice. Lexington Books: Lexington, MA.

Monahan, J. (1981) Predicting violent behavior: An assessment of clinical techniques. Sage: Beverly Hills, CA.

Moos, R.H. (1973) Conceptualizations of human environments. American Psychologist, 28, 652-665.

Panton, J.H. (1958) MMPI profile configurations among crime

classification groups. Journal of Clinical Psychology, 14, 305-308.

Pasternack, S.A. (1975) Violence and victims. Spectrum: New York.

Persons, R.W. & Marks, P.A. (1971) The violent 4-3 MMPI personality type. Journal of Consulting and Clinical Psychology, 36, 189-196.

Pollak, O. (1950) The criminology of women. University of Pennsylvania Press: Philadelphia.

Rubin, B. (1972) Prediction of dangerousness in mentally ill criminals. Archives of General Psychiatry, 72, 397-407.

Sampselle, C.M. (1992) Violence against women: Nursing research, education, and practice issues. Hemisphere: New York.

Shah, S.A. (1978) Dangerousness: A paradigm for exploring some issues in law and psychology. American Psychologist, 33, 224-238.

Simon, R.J. (1975) The contemporary woman and crime. National Institute of Mental Health: Rockville, MD.

Smart, C. (1977) Women, crime, and criminology. Routledge & Kegan Paul: London.

Stuart, R.B. (1981) Violent behavior: Social learning approaches to prediction and treatment. Brunner/Mazel: New York.

Supreme Court of the United States (1987) McCleskey versus Kemp. United States Reports (whole no. 84-6811): Washington, D.C.

Valzelli, L., & Morgese, L. (1981) Aggression and violence: A psycho/biological and clinical approach. Edizioni Centro Culturale E Congressi Saint Vincent: Rome.

Wasieleski, D.T. (1990) A comparison of child molesters and men who commit incest with special reference to dangerousness. Senior honors thesis, Emory University.

Wechsler, D. (1955) Wechsler Adult Intelligence Scale. Psychological Corporation: New York.

Weis, J. (1978) Liberation and crime: The invention of the new female criminal. In P. Wickman & P. Whitten (Eds), Readings in Criminology. Heath: Lexington, MA.

Wenk, E.A., Robinson, J.O., and Smith, G.W. (1972) Can violence be predicted? Crime and Delinquency, 18, 393-402.

West, D.J. (1968) Homosexuality. Aldine: Chicago.

Wolfgang, M.E., & Ferracuti, F. (1970) The subculture of violence. In M.E. Wolfgang, L. Savitz, & N. Johnston (Eds), The sociology of crime and delinquency. Wiley: New York.

Author Index

Subject Index

About the Author

Alfred B. Heilbrun Jr. received the Ph.D. degree from the University of Iowa in 1954 and joined that university's faculty in 1956. He was awarded Diplomate status in 1960 by the American Board of Professional Psychology with a specialty in clinical psychology. Dr. Heilbrun joined the faculty of Emory University in 1965 where he directed the clinical psychology training program and the community-oriented Psychological Center. He retired in 1991 as Distinguished Research Professor of Psychology and continues to serve as a consultant to the Georgia Board of Pardons and Paroles.